INSIGHT POCKET GUIDE

ALGARVE

KU-242-120

APA PUBLICATIONS

Part of the Langenscheidt Publishing Group

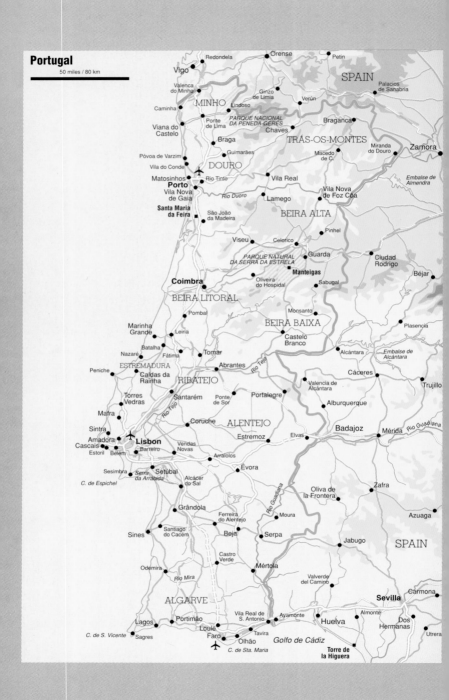

Portugal

50 miles / 80 km

Welcome!

This guidebook combines the interests and enthusiasms of two of the world's best-known information providers: Insight Guides, who have set the standard for visual travel guides since 1970, and Discovery Channel, the world's premier source of non-fiction television programming. Insight Guides' correspondent, Susie Boulton, has devised 19 itineraries to help you make the most of a short stay in the region.

The Algarve stretches from the River Guadiana in the southeast of Portugal to Cape St Vincent in the southwest. Although it covers only about 150 km (95 miles), it is an area of dramatic contrasts. The great divide is the N125 highway, running the length of the region; north of this road are whitewashed villages set amidst orchards of almond and olive trees, while south of it are famous resorts, beaches, golf courses and sports centres. The itineraries in this book start in the west and work through to the east, and include something to suit all tastes, whether it's a morning in a museum, a day deep-sea fishing or a night in a casino. Following the itineraries are ideas on eating out, nightlife, shopping and sports, plus a section of practical information.

Susie Boulton owes her love for the Algarve to her family's skill in water divining. At a time when the area was still considered Europe's best-kept secret, her grandmother and uncle discovered a spring near Albufeira. They built a couple of houses in the little oasis, then later sold up and moved to the hills of Monchique. The stunning view from the summit of Fóia, over lush valleys and hills down to the sea, was Susie's first and most lasting memory of the region. Though things have changed enormously since then, she says the old spirit still lives on.

C O N T E N T S

Pages 8/9: obstinate but traditional transport

Dining, Nightlife, Shopping & Sport

Ideas on where to eat, stay out late and shop as well as a guide to the sporting facilities of the region **68–84**

Calendar of Events

A listing of what's worth watching out for in the Algarve **86–8**

Practical Information

All the background information you will need, including climate, customs and accommodation **90–9**

Maps

Index and Credits 100–103

HISTORY

The Crescent and The Cross

Disembark from a boat and step out on to the streets of Olhão, and you might well assume you are in a Moorish town in North Africa. The windowless ground floors of the houses, the exterior staircases leading to the rooftops and the pierced chimneys are all eloquent evidence of the influence of Moorish ideas in the town. Yet if you were dropped unsuspecting in the old town of Faro or in front of the cathedral at Silves, you would probably think you were in the mainstream of European Christian culture. This contrast illustrates the essence of the Algarve's history and culture. A Moorish province for over 500 years, it then became part of Christian Europe while retaining its Moorish characteristics.

The Algarve has suffered destruction and decay countless times over the centuries. The sumptuous Moorish capital of Silves, then 'ten times more remarkable than Lisbon', fell into ruin after its final capture by the Christians in 1249. In 1587 (when Portugal was under Spanish rule), Sir Francis Drake attacked Lagos and sacked Sagres, devastating its oldest buildings; nine years later Faro was sacked by the Earl of Essex. But the most destructive forces of all have been earthquakes. By far the worst was the great quake of 1755. At 9.30 on the morning of All Saints' Day, when the churches and chapels of Lisbon were packed with local people at prayer, the tremors were so violent that the city rolled like a ship at sea. Churches and houses cracked and

Sancho I, King of Algarve; Silves Castle

Great quake, 1755

split and, in a matter of minutes, Lisbon was laid ruin. The resulting tidal wave was felt in England that afternoon and as far away as the Caribbean that evening. Much of what made up the Algarve was wiped out at a stroke.

What the earthquakes could never shatter, however, was southern Portugal's role as the fulcrum of a seafaring nation. A province whose south-facing coast stretches for some 150 km (95 miles), its relationship with the sea is tightly woven into its history. The Algarve may not play a great role in world events today, but it was from here that the first explorers embarked on the daring voyages which led to the making of the Portuguese empire. For centuries fishing has been a major industry here, and fortunes have been made from tuna and sardines.

The first to take advantage of the abundance of the sea's harvest were the Phoenicians, who set up trading posts in the Algarve some 3,000 years ago and salt-cured sardines and tuna for export. The Celts, Greeks and Carthaginians all had brief spells of occupation but after the Second Punic War (202 BC), the old province of Lusitania (roughly the area comprising modern Portugal) was – despite stout resistance by the population under the much celebrated shepherd hero, Viriatus – progressively brought under Rome's control. The best-preserved evidence of Rome's presence in the Algarve are the ruins of Milreu at Estói (Itinerary 13), where you can still see the remains and mosaics of a grandiose villa and baths, once thought to be part of Ossonoba, Roman Faro.

The Romans held sway until the early part of the 5th century. With the break-up of their empire in the west came the invasion of barbarian tribes. Suevi, Alans and Vandals swept over Lusitania, only to be extinguished in their turn by the Visigoths, who came as agents of the Romans and made their seat at the once Roman town of Ossonoba (Faro).

It was the Moors who really left their mark on the Algarve. In AD 711 they sailed over from Ceuta (North Africa) and within three or four years had taken over a large part of the Iberian peninsula. Moors, mainly of Egyptian stock, soon colonised the Algarve and called it *Al-Gharb,* or 'land of the west'. New skills were brought to the land. Waterwheels were introduced, land was irrigated, rice was planted and almond trees and citrus fruits began to flourish. Craft industries prospered, and skilled artisans worked metal, leather and textiles. Christians had their own civil laws and lived cheek-by-jowl with the Moors. Some of those who worked the land continued to do so, but ceased to own it and instead paid rent to Moorish landlords.

The southern seat of the Moorish kingdom was Silves. It was a sumptuous stronghold with elegant bazaars, mosques, shipyards and a navigable port where ships loaded up with cork and citrus fruits. The castle is now no more than a noble shell. But as you approach the town from the south or east, through rich groves of fruit trees,

Moorish-influenced tiles

and see the mighty turrets crowning the town, you can understand why the Moorish rulers regarded this as their earthly paradise.

Apart from the castle, little else concrete survives to tell the tale of Moorish hegemony. But the dynamics are still there. Inland you can still see artisans hammering out copper and brass, craftsmen hand painting ceramics and old ladies working at lace, linen and embroidery. The most vivid Moorish architectural feature that still survives in the Algarve is the pierced chimney. Other Arabic features are the cubistic houses, interior courtyards and (particularly in the port of Olhão) exterior staircases leading to flat-topped roofs where fishermen's wives used to look out to sea on stormy days.

Despite the duration of the Moorish domination in the south, the Christian resistance began as early as 718 with a military victory at Covadonga in the small kingdom of the Asturias. However, it was not until 1139, with Afonso Henriques' victory at Ourique, that any substantial headway was made. In the same year he became the first King of Portugal and, in 1147, seized the stronghold of Lisbon from the Moors with the help of north European crusaders. His successor, Sancho I, continued the anti-Muslim military campaign and began exerting pressure in the Algarve.

In 1189 Sancho persuaded some of the Christians making up the Third Crusade (with some English among them) to assist his fleet in expelling the Moors from Silves. They anchored off the city on the River Arade (then navigable), beseiged the fortress and forced the city to capitulate. The Moors, numbering about 30,000, fled and the Crusaders proceeded to loot and plunder despite Sancho's protests. The 'victory' is recalled today by the statue of Sancho in the castle, captioned 'King of Silves, the Algarve and Portugal'. Silves was recaptured by the Moors two years later but Sancho's successors, Afonso II and III, reasserted Christian rule. Tavira was taken in 1239 and Faro and Silves ten years later, at which time the Algarve became part of the nation of Portugal. Christianity took over but the spirit in which it is practised here today – with as much superstition as faith, and an abundance of lavish gilt statuary and carving – demonstrates a survival of the Arab mentality.

Following Moorish rule, the principal threat to Portugal and the Algarve was Castile. The climax of the conflict was the celebrated battle of Aljubarotta in 1385, when the Portuguese, under the then 'Defender of the Realm', João of the House of Aviz, crushed their adversary. The victor became King João I of Portugal and married Philippa of

AZULEJOS

It is thanks to the Moors that Portugal is so liberally endowed with glazed tiles, or *azulejos*. The name probably derives from the Arabic *Al Zulaicha,* or *Zuleija,* meaning ceramic mosaic. Other influences were painters from France, Italy and Germany, as well as Portugal's maritime expansion.

Formerly a vogue among the affluent – there used to be a proverb to the effect that it was a poor man who lived in a house without tiles – they are nowadays classless, decorating facades seen on churches and chapels, villas and mansions, park benches and railway stations, and adorning even the simplest dwellings.

Mass production began after the 1755 earthquake, but small family businesses using old methods of tilemaking continued, and still exist today. A fine example of the craft is in the church of São Lourenço (Almansil), whose interior walls and dome are entirely faced with stunning blue-and-white tiles depicting scenes from the life of St Lawrence. Other examples are the tiled stairways in the gardens of the villa at Estói and the scenes from the life of St Francis in the Church of São Francisco in Faro.

Lancaster, daughter of John of Gaunt (hence the foundation of the great Anglo-Portuguese alliance, formalised by the Treaty of Windsor in 1386 and unbroken to this day). The royal couple's third son, Henry, was to play a vital role in world history in years to come.

Henry the Navigator and Manuel the Fortunate

Henry the Navigator was probably spurred on by mixed motives: a love of Christ and a love of commerce. At an early age he was appointed Master of the Order of Christ (the old Knights Templar), but most of all he is remembered as the catalyst for the great discoveries. In 1415, at the age of 21, Henry began to campaign for revenge against the Moors. He and his brothers led a successful expedition to Ceuta, taking the city for the Portuguese crown. By 1427 Portuguese ships had landed in the Canaries and Azores. In the 1440s Henry was sending out the discoverers in new ships called caravels, powered by sail alone. Built and fitted out in Lagos, they sailed from there to the Cape Verde Islands and, according to Henry's will, 'into the land of Guinea three hundred leagues'. If this was the case, they had gone beyond the most westerly point of what is now the African coast.

FISHING IN THE ALGARVE

As early as 1353 Edward III granted the fishermen of the Algarve rights by treaty to fish cod off the coast of England. At the turn of the 15th century the Corte Real brothers voyaged to Greenland, Newfoundland and Nova Scotia and, from then on, Portuguese ships began to harvest cod as far afield as Newfoundland. Dried salted cod became the staple dish and, despite the abundance of delicious fresh fish in local waters, it remains one of the most popular Portuguese dishes.

By the 18th century the fishing industry was so well established in the Algarve that the dynamic Marquês de Pombal set up a chartered company to control the sardine and tuna fishing industries in the province. Vila Real de Santo António was constructed as a model fishing port.

The hunting of tuna fish is a centuries-old tradition, probably first introduced by the Sicilians and Genoese. Until relatively recently, the fish (weighing anything up to 450 kg/992 lbs) were caught in nets, killed by a team of harpooners and gaffed and hoisted on board. The bloody battles that took place in the water between the tuna and the harpooners were aptly described as 'bullfights of the sea'. Today the methods have changed and tuna fishing takes place only on the high seas. Many of the fish, particularly the smaller ones, are eaten fresh, and others are preserved in vegetable oil and exported worldwide.

Fishing communities still thrive in the Algarve. Portimão is one of the world's most important towns for fish canning, though sadly you can no longer see the catch being offloaded at the quayside. The Maritime Museum in Faro is an absorbing place for anyone interested in the Algarve's fishing, past and present. For those who want a more practical slant, there are fishing trips of every variety, pursuing anything from the humble sardine to the dramatic mako shark *(see Itinerary 5)*.

Vasco da Gama

What Henry set in motion was carried on by Dias when he rounded the Cape of Good Hope in 1488, by Vasco da Gama when he discovered the East Indies in the late 1490s and by Cabral when, in 1500, he sailed across the Atlantic and discovered Brazil, the 'jewel in the crown' of the Portuguese Empire.

When Manuel I came to the throne in 1495 he reaped the profits of those heady days of expansion. His ships brought back every kind of exotica known to the East and to Brazil, and the vessels were seen as the lifeblood of the nation. Conscious of the fact that he was the wealthiest ruler in Europe, he styled himself as 'Lord of the Navigation, Conquest and Commerce of Ethiopia, Arabia, Persia and India' and, for good reason, was nicknamed 'Manuel the Fortunate'. Architectural styles began to mirror the glorious maritime era and the king gave his name to the new movement, 'Manueline'. This was a kind of maritime form characterised by fine, often exuberant decoration inspired by nautical features, by the flora and fauna of the East and by the legends brought back by the discoverers.

Fluctuating Fortunes

A little over half a century after Manuel's death, the nation suffered a devastating blow at the hands of King Sebastião. Having succeeded to the throne at a tender age, he turned out to be an arrogant and opiniated youth, convinced that his mission in life was to be some kind of 'Captain of Christ' against the infidels. Even as a teenager he attempted (unsuccessfully) to incite the Algarvian nobility to join in a crusade. However, his opportunity came at last when the ruler of Fez was thrown out and appealed to him for help. He mustered a motley army, set sail from Lagos and landed at Arzila in North Africa. Four days later, on 4 August 1578 at Alcacer-Quibir, his hot and hungry men had no option but to join battle with a vastly stronger Moroccan force. In this 'Battle of the Three Kings', nearly 15,000 men were captured or killed and only around 100 escaped with their lives.

With Sebastião perished the flower of the Portuguese aristocracy. The royal line was weakened and in 1580 the Spanish annexed the Portuguese crown. Sixty years of Spanish rule followed, during which period Sir Francis Drake attacked Lagos and sacked Sagres, (destroying in the process the old house of Henry the Navigator). The Earl of Essex also launched an attack and burned down Faro,

having first seized the library of the Bishop, which he gave to Sir Thomas Bodley for the library he had founded in Oxford.

In 1640 the Braganza dynasty was established, bringing an end to Spanish rule. It was to last until 1910 when the Republic was founded. For a while Portugal was enriched by gold, spices and diamonds: debts were paid off and exuberant baroque architecture flourished. In every town and village you can still see the baroque-style church, with its delicately sloping shoulders, highly ornate doorway and picturesque belfry. The figures may not appeal to northern European eyes, but they are manifestations both of a style of art and a 'style' of faith.

New-found fortunes and lavish baroque architecture were devastated by the Great Earthquake in 1755, in which thousands died. In the wake of the disaster the already powerful Marquês de Pombal, Chief Minister to the Crown, gained almost total political control in Portugal. His methods were ruthless and arbitrary but, in the following 20 years or so, he did much to repair and modernise the country. In the Algarve he rebuilt Vila Real de Santo António in five months and introduced state control of the fishing industry (later discontinued).

The Algarve, along with the rest of Portugal, was occupied by the French during the Peninsula War, and Napoleon planned a Principality of the Algarve. But anti-French feeling was strong in the province and the popular risings in Olhão and Faro in June 1808 were some of the first in the peninsula. An assembly met in Faro and elected a kind of military junta of the Algarve. In 1808 a small group of intrepid fishermen from Olhão sailed in a small caïque across the Atlantic to Brazil to tell the exiled Portuguese king that Napoleon's troops had left his kingdom. Under Generals Beresford and Wellesley (later to become Duke of Wellington), British troops finally forced the French back into Spain in 1811.

Towards a Modern State

The second half of the 18th century saw the gradual rise of republican ideas in Portugal as a whole. Against this growing tide of feeling King Carlos I chose to govern by decree and was assassinated (along with his heir) by fanatics in 1908. Two years later the monarchy was overthrown in favour of a republic and King Manuel II fled to England where he later died.

The Republic failed to bring about popularly anticipated reforms and its life was characterised by strikes, economic problems and general discontent. In 1926 the constitution was suspended and a provisional government was formed. The next decades saw the dramatic rise to power of Dr Antonio de Oliveira Salazar, formerly Professor of Economics at Coimbra University. He progressed from Finance Minister to Prime Minister in 1932, and effectively ruled the country until he suffered a stroke in 1968. Although his monetarist policies brought about budgetary surpluses between 1928–40, it was at the expense of relative isolation from Europe.

Salazar was succeeded in 1968 by Marcelo Caetano, whose policies of liberalisation caused serious discontent within the armed forces. This in turn led to the bloodless Carnation Revolution of 1974 (so-called because of the red carnations in the barrels of the soldiers' rifles). Elections a year later resulted in an impressive socialist victory under Mário Soares. Since then, Socialist or Social Democratic parties have been in power in Portugal and economic stability has always been of paramount importance. The initial period of EC membership brought economic growth, new middle-class wealth, lower inflation and a drop in unemployment. There was a temporary slowing down in 1993; however, Portugal's commitment to European integration was crowned in 1998 with qualification for entry into the single European currency. The successful Expo '98 crowned a great year.

Geography

The Algarve stretches 150 km (95 miles) from the River Guadiana in the east – a natural frontier with Spain – to Cape St Vincent in the west. East of Faro the Sotavento is a flat stretch of coast with offshore islets and sandy beaches. To the west, the coast is typified by cliffs and wide sandy beaches. West of Albufeira is a varied coastline, with fantastic rock formations, grottoes and coves culminating in the windswept Sagres peninsula. Behind the coast is a parched landscape of olive, almond and citrus trees, but only a short way inland eucalyptus, cork, carob, fig and other fruit trees abound and hillsides are covered in rock roses and wild flowers. The Serra de Monchique, dividing the western part of the Algarve from the Alentejo, is green and hilly with wooded slopes and luxuriant vegetation.

CORK

Open any bottle of wine and the chances are the cork comes from Portugal. Over half the world's supply is produced here and you won't have to drive far in the Algarve to spot the cork oak. The tree is easily recognised by its broad, rounded head and glossy-green, holly-like leaves, or by the raw red trunk visible where the bark has been stripped off. Cork oaks live for between 150–200 years and must mature for 25 years before the first stripping of the outer bark takes place. Each tree yields between 60–100 pounds of cork in one cutting. The layer gradually grows again and strippings then take place every nine years, the quality of the cork improving each year. Inland you can often see piles of cork by the roadside or large slabs piled high on carts or lorries, en route to one of the 600 cork factories in Portugal. The virgin cork is fit only for floors, floats or decorative purposes: the superior cork in your bottle will be from the second or subsequent strippings.

Historical Outline

1000–500 BC Phoenicians set up trading posts and colonies in the Algarve.

700–500 Celts settle, heralding the beginning of the Iron Age.

202 Carthaginian Algarvian enclaves pass to the Romans after the Second Punic War.

202–137 Subjugation by the Romans and annexation of Lusitania (roughly modern Portugal).

AD 406–18 Barbarian tribes sweep over Iberia, including the Algarve.

418 Visigoths take Ossonoba (later known as Faro).

469 Visigoths effectively establish their own kingdom in Portugal, including the Algarve.

711 Portugal invaded by Moors and is quickly overrun. Last Visigothic military resistance at Merida (713) and Ossonoba (taken in about 714).

8th century Relics of the 4th-century martyr St Vincent brought to the sacred promontory of Cape St Vincent.

1064 County of Coimbra established by Ferdinand, Count of Castile.

1095 Afonso VI, now of Leon and Castile, entrusts his son-in-law, Henry of Burgundy, with the enlarged County of Coimbra, now called 'Portucale'.

1114 Afonso Henriques declares an independent nation of Portugal from Minho to Modego, with Coimbra as the capital.

1147 Afonso and Crusaders finally conquer the Moorish stronghold of Lisbon.

1173 St Vincent's relics taken to Lisbon. Legend has it that the boat bore a raven fore and aft which became the crest of Lisbon.

1185 Sancho I begins conquest of the remaining Moslem kingdom in the south.

1189 Crusaders under Sancho I capture Silves. Sancho declared 'King of Portugal, Silves and the Algarve'.

1191 Silves recaptured by Moors from Africa.

1239 Christian forces enter Tavira.

1248 On succeeding to the Crown, Afonso III musters forces for a campaign to take the Algarve.

1249 Faro and Silves taken, effectively marking the end of Moorish hegemony in the Algarve.

1385 Fernando I dies, ending the Burgundian dynasty. Juan I of Castile prepares to invade, whereupon João of the House of Aviz is appointed as Defender of the Realm. João of Aviz routs Castilians at the battle of Aljubarrota and becomes King João I. He then marries Philippa, daughter of John of Gaunt.

1386 The Treaty of Windsor formalises the alliance between England and Portugal.

1415 Portuguese under Henry the Navigator take Ceuta. This marks the beginning of Portuguese colonial expansion.

1488 Diaz rounds the Cape of Good Hope.

1495 Manuel I takes over the Portuguese throne.

1497–8 Vasco da Gama opens the sea routes to India.

1500 Cabral discovers Brazil and the Spice Islands.

1520 Magellan sets out on his voyage to circumnavigate the globe.

1557 The young Sebastião ascends to the throne.

1577 Seat of diocese of Algarve transferred from Silves to Faro.

1578 Sebastião's crusade to Morocco and his defeat and death at the Battle of the Three Kings.

1580 Portugal, annexed by Philip II, becomes a Spanish province.

1587 Drake attacks the Algarve during the Spanish War.

1596 The English under the Earl of Essex sack Faro.

1640 Spanish rule is ended by a nationalist revolution under the Duke of Bragança, later to become King João IV.

1662 Catherine of Bragança marries Charles II of England. Tangier and Bombay are part of her dowry.

1755 The Great Earthquake destroys Lisbon and wreaks havoc over much of the Algarve.

1807 Napoleonic forces under Junot enter Portugal and the royal family flee to Brazil in English ships.

1808 Peninsula War begins, the Portuguese army supporting Wellington. Sixteenth of June civil uprising at Olhão is followed by one at Faro setting up a Provincial Junta of the Algarve.

1810 Massena is prevented from entering Lisbon by the lines of Torres Vedras.

1811 French leave Portugal.

1832–4 War of the Two Brothers, between Miguel (Liberals) and Pedro (Absolutists) for the Crown. Miguel's navy helped by the English off Cape St Vincent. Faro, a liberal headquarters, is beseiged by Absolutists.

1903 Treaty of Windsor is publicly reaffirmed during a visit by Edward VII to Portugal.

1908 King Carlos assassinated by liberal fanatics.

1910 Portugal declared a republic. Manuel II is forced to abdicate and flees to England.

1926 The Gomes da Costa dictatorship begins, followed by *coup d'état,* after which Carmona becomes president.

1928 Salazar is appointed as the Minister of Finance to restore economic order.

1932 Salazar becomes Prime Minister, retaining financial portfolio.

1939–45 Neutral Portugal leases the Azores to the USA, thereby helping to break the German submarine campaign on Anglo-American shipping lines.

1968 Salazar retires and Marcelo Caetano takes over and begins a policy of liberalisation.

1974 MFA (Armed Forces Movement) overthrows government in bloodless revolution. Some 700,000 refugees from newly independent former colonies pour into Portugal.

1976 A constitution is drawn up based on universal suffrage and a single legislative chamber. Socialists win election and Dr Mário Soares becomes Prime Minister of a minority government.

1986 Portugal becomes a member of the EC. Mário Soares, three times socialist prime minister, becomes its first non-military president.

1994 Lisbon chosen as Europe's cultural capital.

1998 Portugal hosts Expo '98 and qualifies for entry to the single European currency.

2004 Portugal due to host the European Football Championships.

Ocean

**Algarve
Route map**

12 km / 7,5 miles

All heights in meters

1. World's End – The Sagres Peninsula

Salema beach for breakfast and morning dip; Sagres peninsula and Cape St Vincent; afternoon on an unspoilt beach.

It is no surprise that this gaunt, windswept promontory was once known as the *Fim do Mundo*. Waves crash against giant cliffs, aloes bow to the winds and fig trees huddle against the barren land. Take the modern houses away and you can imagine why this south-western tip of continental Europe was believed by the great discoverers to be the end of the world. It was here that the half-English Henry the Navigator mustered together the most famous cartographers, boat builders and mariners to plot the famous voyages that were to found the Portuguese Empire. In true Algarvian style, Sagres has a meagre supply of tourist information. Brush up on your history first if you want to get the most out of this major landmark.

Start the day on the sweeping beach at **Salema** with an early morning dip or a gentle jog along the sands. Watch the fishermen drag the skiffs up the beach, laying out their morning's catch and washing squid on the sands. The **Miramar** beach bar (open from 9am), just off the narrow street of fishermen's houses running parallel to the beach, offer continental or cooked breakfasts: you can sit on the bamboo terrace overlooking the sea while you eat, a perfect way to start the day.

By the time the tourists start to arrive on the beach (10–10.30am) you should be heading west. Join the main N125 and turn left towards Sagres. Just 2 km (1¼ miles) after the village of Figueira look out on the right for the **Chapel of Guadalupe**, a delightful little church where Henry the Navigator used to pray for help on his planned routes to distant lands. He lived for a while at Raposeira, a sleepy village further along the main road. You can see the house if you wish (ask at the cafe in the square for instructions), but it looks neither old nor remarkable.

Stop briefly at **Vila do Bispo** to admire the blue-and-gold extravaganza in the baroque church. Ask the sacristan to switch on the lights so that you can see the fine blue-and-white *azulejos* depicting a whole range of secular motifs, the painted wood ceiling and the chancel in gilded wood. If you are hungry, the cafe Correia is in the street roughly running opposite the church. Barnacles (*percebes*) are the speciality here.

Rejoin the main road, which now runs over a windswept plateau, where plants are sparse and trees are stunted. Drive through the straggling outskirts of Sagres, typified by squat roadside homes advertising *quartos* (rooms). When you reach the town, follow the sign for the **Fortaleza**, whose awesome walls will soon loom on the horizon. Drive over the narrow peninsula, through the tunnel-like fortified gateway and park inside the fortress.

It was here that Henry the Navigator is said to have set up his famous School of Navigation, but only a small white domed chapel now survives from that era. Use your imagination to picture the great marine think-tank and the caravels coming round the cape with their booty from distant lands. What may be original is the

Fishermen on Salema beach

large *rosa do ventos*, a type of mariners' compass, that you can see on the left as you come into the fortress. It was only discovered in 1928 and still looks somewhat weed-infested and forgotten. The construction of a concrete, bunker-like Museum within the fortress walls has been the subject of national controversy, now referred to by architects as the 'Sagren Syndrome'.

Take the track to the right, past the peeling white facade of the small domed chapel (where Henry probably worshipped) and follow the route skirting the edge of the cliffs. You can go by foot if it is not too gusty and you have the stamina. Stop at the tip of the promontory near the red-topped lighthouse and watch weather-beaten fishermen, perched on precarious ledges, casting their lines into the rough seas below. Fish for dinner is taken home in wicker baskets lodged on the back of scooters, with long rods towering above. There are beautiful views (weather permitting) of the lighthouse at Cape of St Vincent to the west, the cliffs to the east and out to the infinite ocean.

You can get a better view of **Cape St Vincent** by taking the main N268 westward (the road is marked to the Cabo de São Vicente at the Sagres roundabout). Drive over the wind-battered plateau for 6 km (3¾ miles). Before reaching the cape you'll see on the left the old fortress of Belixe (now a restaurant) and an old chapel. On arrival at the cape, there is space to park near the stalls selling fishermen's socks and chunky sweaters. The lighthouse sits at the tip of the promontory, surrounded by neat gardens and spectacular sea vistas. Here you can watch ocean-going vessels rounding the cape from the lookout point to the right of the lighthouse and the sea breakers crashing into the cliffs 70 metres (230 ft) below. Visits inside the lighthouse are, it seems, entirely dependent on the mood of the keeper on duty. It is best to try to join on the tail of a

visiting group; if the door to the lighthouse (at the end of the pathway) is shut, track down a keeper and try your powers of persuasion. The interior is imposing: massive crystal, gleaming brass and 3,000 Watt bulbs. The lantern, designed and made in France, is the biggest in Europe, with a light visible from a distance of 90 km (56 miles).

Return to Sagres for a lobster lunch overlooking the port. At the main roundabout go straight on, then turn right when you see the Hotel Baleeira. This brings you down to the port and the **A Tasca Restaurant** (tel: 282-624177, closed Saturday). Converted from the old market, it is full of character and has first-class fresh fish, much of which is caught on the restaurant's own boat. Specialities are lobster and *amêijoas na cataplana* (clams in cataplana). You can eat outside on the sea view terrace or in the large interior, complete with oven for smoking fish. After lunch, if a boat trip to see the coast and grottoes appeals to you, ask down at the port.

The gorgeous **Praia do Zavial** is an uncrowded beach on the south coast. If you want a taste of the real Atlantic, the dramatic **Praia do Castelejo** (northwest of Vila do Bispo) is an alternative.

For Zavial, return to Raposeira, take the right turn marked Ingrina and Hortas do Tabula and bump over the potholed track for 1km (½ mile); fork left and the beach is 3 km (1¾ miles) further on. For Praia do Castelejo return to Vila do Bispo and, just before the centre, turn left down the road marked Praia do Castelejo. A rough, narrow road brings you down to a sweeping beach with golden sands. Brave the waters (beware of strong currents), then take a refreshing evening drink on the panoramic terrace of the beach bar. On a warm evening this is a lovely spot to dine on the local speciality *arroz de peixe* (rice with fish) and watch the sun set.

The Fort at Sagres

Unspoilt beaches

2. Sun and Surf – West Coast Beaches

Leisurely breakfast at the pousada in Sagres; trip up the west coast, exploring unspoilt beaches; early evening at Aljezur; sunset from Cape St Vincent or Sagres.

Winds, waves and coolish waters keep the majority of holiday-makers off the Algarve's west coast. What they miss is a series of wild, stunningly beautiful beaches, many only accessible via dirt tracks or by foot.

Start the day in Sagres and treat yourself to breakfast at the **Pousada do Infante**. One of the only two state-sponsored hotels in the Algarve (and currently being refurbished), the Do Infante is stylish and civilised with lush lawns, spacious rooms and a prime cliff-top location looking across the rugged coast to the *fortaleza*. Although breakfast here will set you back 1,250$, it is more ample than most. Before leaving Sagres, why not watch some of the morning's fishing activity down at the **port** and **market** (turn right at the main road and right again at the Hotel Baleeira), and visit the **Fortaleza**, where Henry the Navigator is said to have set up his navigation school and plotted his great expeditions.

Leave Sagres by mid to late morning and make for the west coast via the small town of Vila do Bispo. Take the main N268 out of Sagres and as you come into Vila do Bispo take the left turning to **Praia do Castelejo**. A rough, narrow road takes you to one of the more accessible (but still beautiful) beaches on the west coast. The sweeping sands, high cliffs and hinterland of hilly moors carpeted in wild flowers make a splendid sight. You can brave the waves, walk the cliff tops or just sit at the beach bar terrace.

Your next stop is **Carrapateira**, further north. The only way to get there is to return to Vila do Bispo, turn left onto the main

N125 and left again just after the village, marked to Aljezur. The road is potholed but traffic-free with wayside eucalyptus trees and pines arching over the road. The village of Carrapateira is little more than a jumble of houses on steep cobbled streets, a tiny market-place and a handful of bars with resting backpackers and thirsty surfers. What really makes the place are the beaches. See them on a fine day and it is hard to believe that such beauty spots, with their sweeps of sand, dramatic surf and cliffs, are still undiscovered. The only people on the beach are likely to be a handful of surfers or latter-day hippies soaking up the sun.

To get to the first beach, **Amado**, take the first turn left after the *Escola Primaria* (primary school) that you see above the road as you come into Carrapateira. The distance to the beach is about 2 km (1¼ miles), along a dirt track and through a natural park. Pass the Pensão Valentin (nice rustic French-run B&B) after about 200 metres (650 ft) and follow the road until it reaches a fork where you bear left. This is where the spectacular views of cliffs and sea begin. About 250 metres (820 ft) before you come to the beach, watch out for a shack marked *Restaurante*. Don't be deterred by shabby appearances – Manuel António's cafe has excellent grilled fish or chicken, good sea views and a friendly atmosphere. Service is very laid back, so specify a time for your lunch, order it and come back later. Meanwhile, make the most of the beach, with its beautiful stretch of sand and dunes. If you bathe, watch out for currents and sizable waves. Off season, you can walk in peace along the cliffs and enjoy splendid sea views. In spring pretty wild flowers of all colours grow in the stony soil.

Cape St Vincent

Don't leave Carrapateira without taking at least a brief look at the staggeringly beautiful beach of **Bordeira** a little further up. Go back to the main road, turn left and very soon left again, along another dusty dirt track. Drive for around 2 km (1¼ miles) past dusty cacti and fig trees, and you will see down to your right a dramatic sweep of beach, dunes and cliffs. Further up the hill there are even better views, where a lone goatherd may be sitting on the cliffs with his brown-speckled goats.

Leave Carrapateira by late afternoon and rejoin the N268 for the town of **Aljezur**. The road cuts inland, through deserted hilly territory to Alfambras. Ignore the road here to Lagos and go straight on to Aljezur. When you get to the centre of the town, turn right over the bridge, park by the marketplace/tourist office and make your way up by foot to the castle *(see Itinerary 7)*. Depending on the time and the whereabouts of your base, either take the main road south to Lagos or retrace your steps along the west coast to watch the sun sink at Cape St Vincent or Sagres. If you want to stay in the area for dinner, try the excellent A Tasca Restaurant at Sagres port *(see Itinerary 1)*, which is open until 10pm.

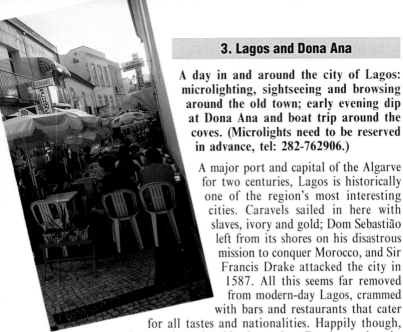

Lagos

3. Lagos and Dona Ana

A day in and around the city of Lagos: microlighting, sightseeing and browsing around the old town; early evening dip at Dona Ana and boat trip around the coves. (Microlights need to be reserved in advance, tel: 282-762906.)

A major port and capital of the Algarve for two centuries, Lagos is historically one of the region's most interesting cities. Caravels sailed in here with slaves, ivory and gold; Dom Sebastião left from its shores on his disastrous mission to conquer Morocco, and Sir Francis Drake attacked the city in 1587. All this seems far removed from modern-day Lagos, crammed with bars and restaurants that cater for all tastes and nationalities. Happily though, culture and tourism blend together. Despite earthquake devastation and, more recently, the concrete sprawl, there is still an elegance about the central streets and squares, and sufficient historical landmarks to ensure that the past survives.

For a bird's eye view of the whole bay, take to the skies in a **microlight** with long distance world record holders Gerry and Manuela Breen. The aerodrome lies on the main N125 north of town (open 10am–1pm daily, closed Sunday). A ten-minute trip at 9,500$00 will take you round the bay; 20-minute trips down to Burgau cost 16,500$00 (no photos allowed).

Spend the rest of the morning in Lagos centre, starting at the main square, Praça Infante Dom Henrique (confusingly also called the Praça da República). In summer, parking can be a problem and you may have to cruise up and down the harbour side road for a while until you find a space.

From the square with its gardens and cafe you can pinpoint a number of historical landmarks. Look first at the large bronze statue of **Henry the Navigator**, appropriately looking seaward, sextant in hand. As governor he lived in the **Castelo dos Governadores** on the west side of the square. Facing the statue and to your left in the distance is the old fort which defended the entrance to the port in the 17th century. On the south side of the square the **Church of Santa Maria** is unremarkable except from some good 18th-century wooden statuary. More or less opposite the insignificant arcade under the Lagos Customs House is the site of the **Mercado dos Escravos,** where the hapless African slaves used to be sold.

Take the cobbled Rua Henrique Correia de Silva (near the church) up to the museum and **Chapel of Santo António**. The plain facade belies the most lavish ecclesiastical interior of the Algarve and one of the very few to survive the 1755 earthquake. The walls are almost entirely faced with intricately carved gilded woodwork. The entrance to the **Regional Museum** is on the right (open, like the church, daily 9.30am–12.30pm and 2–5pm, Mon and holidays excepted). The first section is devoted to archaeological finds from all over the Algarve; then there's a more extended ethnographic section with all things Algarvian: sardine nets, lobster pots, pierced chimneys and farming implements, plus some oddities preserved in bottles, such as a one-eyed sheep and two-headed cat. Labelling as usual is in Portuguese only but the staff speak a smattering of English.

Exiting the museum/church turn right down the Rua da Silves Lopes, which leads into the hub of central Lagos: Rua 25 de Abril. Stop at **Casa do Papagaio**, Nos. 27 and 29 on your right, where a couple of loquacious parrots catch the eye of passers-by and lure them into a dark and fascinating treasure trove of Portuguese antiques. The shop sells everything from coins and cash tills to African statuary. The **Restaurante Sebastião** (tel: 282-762795) is almost opposite, pricey by local standards but a favourite with foreigners because of its location, open-air terrace and variety of food.

Fork left at the end of the street, proceed past the tourist office and into Praça Gil Eanes, named after the first explorer to round Cape Bojador, a far-flung point on the west coast of the Sahara. Cross the square, casting a glance as you go at the rather provocative

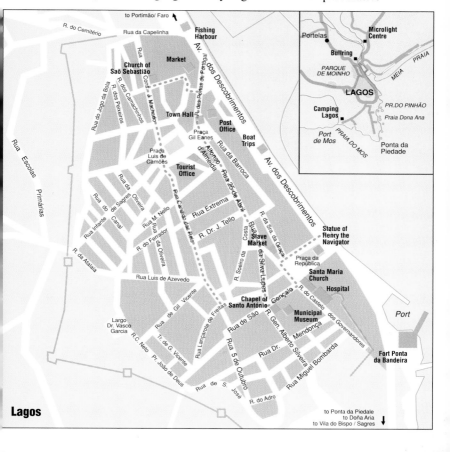

Lagos

statue of the pink-faced Sebastião, a precocious 13-year-old boy. Carry further on, past the gardens and post office on your right, and make for the fish and vegetable market which stands back from the main harbourside road. Just beyond the market there's a good *pastelaria* where you can purchase fancy marzipan cakes, a speciality of the Algarve.

Retrace your steps a little way until you see a flight of steps up to your right. Go to the top, turn right, then wind left and along to the **Church of São Sebastião.** Note the Renaissance portal; the inside (often locked) is embellished with decorative tiles. Come

down the steep Rua Conselheiro Joaquim Machado into the Praça Luís de Camões (named after the Portuguese poet). If you have time, you could browse in the Rua Cândido dos Reis, or explore some of the streets east, going up to the old city walls.

For lunch choose between Sebastião or for somewhere simpler, the **Restaurant Piri Piri** at Rua Afonso d'Almeida near the tourist office. A regional tourist menu here with three courses, wine and coffee costs only 1,500$00.

Linger over lunch, then spend part of the afternoon browsing around **Lagos** at leisure (shops close at 1pm and open again at 3pm). By late afternoon make for the promontory south of the city, where sandy coves and clear grottoes lie beneath weathered cliffs. Either take a boat from the waterfront (3,250$00 per boat, for a 50-minute trip), weather and waves permitting, or drive to the tip of the promontory and get a cheaper trip there. Follow the main road towards Sagres and take the left turning marked for Dona Ana and Ponta da Piedade. At the first fork turn left and follow the road down to the lighthouse, where you can park the car. Take the track to the left over the promontory for a bird's-eye view of the red-tinted rocks eroded into arches, pitted with coves and dotted with squawking gulls that cluster on the rugged ledges. A long flight of steps leads down to small boats which can take you out for a closer look at the grottoes and deep green waters. The sea here is ideal for snorkelling or underwater fishing if you happen to be suitably equipped.

End the day at **Dona Ana** (you'll see it signed to the right as you go back), a small resort with some ugly architecture but a pretty little beach by way of compensation. You can take an early evening dip here, then sip a cocktail and watch the distant fishing smacks and the dark shadows fall over the strange ochre outcrops jutting out of the sea.

4. Portimão and Ferragudo

Portimão for morning shopping and a sardine lunch, followed by a rest at the Praia da Rocha beach then dinner in Ferragudo.

Portimão

The splendid new suspension bridge over the River Avade has relieved the through traffic that has traditionally clogged the streets of Portimão. Although this main town has no monuments of real interest it has the best selection of shops in the Algarve, a bustling harbourside and an abundance of cafes and restaurants serving the catch of the day.

The smell of sardines permeating street corners is a sure indication that this is an active fishing port. Until relatively recently, the key attraction for the tourist was the sight of the fresh fish tossed up in wicker baskets onto the quayside. The landing of the fish now takes place in a closed-off area on the other side of the estuary. Now you are unlikely to see more than an occasional smack coming in with sardines or a fisherman washing and slicing inky squid on the quayside.

Park as near to the old fishing port as you can and browse around the **river quays** where cruisers and trawlers are usually anchored. This is the place to book a day's big-game fishing (see *Itinerary 5, page 34*) or an excursion on a yacht sailing down the coast.

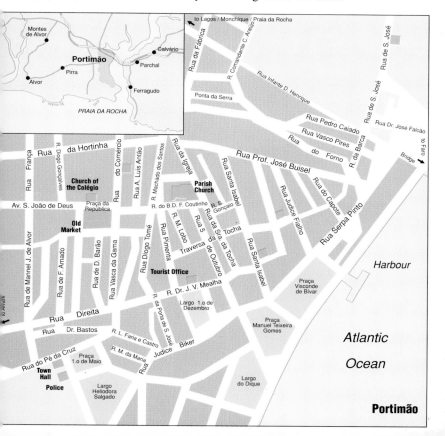

You can stop for coffee in the **public gardens** nearby, then explore the old residential quarter by taking the narrow streets off the Rua Serpa Pinto. **Rua Santa Isabel** is a fascinating old district with up-market shops occupying the ground floors of some of the town's finer houses: No. 5, the **Galeria Portimão**, has stylish modern art; Nos. 8–10 stock antique coins and stamps; No. 26, **Charles Jourdan**, is the place for classic shoes at lower prices than in Paris or London; while No. 32, **Vinda Boutique**, sells hand-crafted gifts.

Two streets to the east, the Rua 5 de Outubro has a further choice of shops. Here you will also find the dominant **parish church**, rebuilt after the 1755 earthquake, but retaining a fine portico from the original building. Make for the square southwest of the church, with the old market at the far side, and take the pedestrianised **Rua do Comércio** leading off the square. This is the main shopping street, so browse around, then make your way back towards the harbour via its extension, the Rua Vasco da Gama. Turn left at the end of the street and along to the **Largo 1 de Dezembro**, a small park with attractively tiled benches depicting the major episodes of Portuguese history.

When the smell of fresh fish on charcoal begins to whet your appetite return to the waterside near the bridge where sardines will be sizzling on grills. Take your pick of these simple cafe-style restaurants and order sardines, salad and a jug of wine. Sardines are at their fattest and best in July, August and September.

Sleep off lunch on the **Praia da Rocha,** the Algarve's most famous

Praia da Rocha

beach. You used to be able to take a horse-drawn cart to the beach, but now it's a case of taking a taxi or bus, or joining the traffic along the dual carriageway to the coast. Be warned though: Praia da Rocha takes the biscuit for crass coastal development. The first resort in the Algarve (with half a dozen hotels and a handful of villas in the 1960s), it is now one long row of Costa-style development. The saving grace is the beach: a superb swath of golden sands, studded with weird rock formations and backed by cliffs sufficiently high to make the cliff top development (once you are on the beach) pale into insignificance. Sunbathe, swim or walk the length of the beach, spotting the sculptural forms along the sands. There are tunnels and arches and rocks which look like bears and humans if you use your imagination.

The old Fortaleza de Santa Catarina at the far eastern end of the resort is the perfect place for an afternoon drink. Bird's-eye views across the estuary and down to the long jetty where hopeful anglers cast their lines compensate for an uninspiring cafe/bar.

The fort at Ferragudo

Your evening port of call is **Ferragudo**, visible across the estuary. It is no distance as the crow flies but unfortunately to get there you have to go via Portimão. Go back into town, cross the main bridge and take the second road on the right. You will soon see the picturesque sight of Ferragudo's houses jostling on the hill, with beached boats on the estuary and lobster pots stacked on the quayside. Stroll around the steep cobbled streets of the centre where cats doze and locals sit in doorways fanning braziers and looking curiously at passers-by. Wander up to the fort for good views over the estuary.

Dine at the **A Lanterna Restaurant** (tel: 282-423948, closed Sunday), on your right as you join the N125 coming out of Ferragudo. The fish soup is excellent; so is the lamb marinaded in rosemary, garlic and mint and the duckling roasted with orange sauce. Pass by the ubiquitous *gelado* or almond tart and end the meal with a special Portuguese cake called *Pão de Ló*.

This itinerary suggests a day's deep sea fishing off a luxury cruiser if you have the inclination and the money.

According to the locals, the waters of the Algarve are the last unspoiled big-game fishing area left in Europe. Join a deep-sea cruise and the likelihood is you will catch a shark or two. Bass, conger and rays are plentiful as are the bottom-dwelling species that you can catch with hand lines while waiting for the big ones to bite. No experience is necessary (professional crew are always at hand to help) but it helps to be a good sailor. Waters are reasonably calm from June to September, but at other times of the year be prepared for rougher seas.

For speed, comfort and the latest in gear, try the Altea or the Agualte (tel: 282-423807) cruisers, both of which operate from Portimão. A full day's fishing currently costs 12,000$. Non-participants, who sit and watch the action from the sundeck, pay 6,000$. Lunch (which is optional) costs an additional 1,000$. Details are available from the harbour at **Portimão** (look out for Lodewijk, the blue-eyed Dutchman who runs the show) or from the **Big Game Fishing Centre** (Cepemar) in the centre of town (tel: 282-425866; fax: 282-425341).

Boats are fully equipped with fighting chairs, outriggers, big game rods and reels; and the latest sonar system enables detection of fish up to a distance of 75 km (48 miles). It takes about two hours to get to the high reefs where the sharks hunt (usually about 20 km (12 miles) from the shore).

Other species likely to be lurking around in the line of fire are the blue shark (slim, deep-blue and potentially dangerous), the copper shark and the streamlined mako, which fights like a marlin and is prized for its speed and dramatic leaps out of the sea. The tastiest of the local sharks, the fish is frequently found served up in local restaurants, masquerading as swordfish.

The biggest of the game are played from the fighting chair and can take anything up to two hours to land. Lodewijk's largest landing was a blue shark of 110 kilos (242 lb 8 oz).

Those dependent on the day's fish for their dinner are in for a disappointment – the whole catch goes to the crew.

6. Peaks of Monchique

Breakfast in the ancient capital of Silves; spa waters, firewater and midday meal at Caldas de Monchique; cobbled streets and convent ruins in the market town of Monchique; panorama from the highest peak in the Algarve

Monchique shepherd

Start your day in **Silves**, the Moorish capital of the Algarve. As you approach the town, the red sandstone walls and turrets of the mighty fortress make a splendid sight. The shell alone provides eloquent evidence that Silves was once far more than a sleepy rural town. Using Itinerary 8 as a guide, breakfast at the **Café Inglês** and see the castle and cathedral. By mid morning take the N124 west through vines and citrus groves, stopping for sweet juicy oranges from roadside vendors. When you arrive at the tiny village of Porto de Lagos (11 km/7 miles), take the right turning signposted to Monchique. Climb up through the foothills of the Serra de Monchique, which is densely wooded and famed for its luxuriant flora.

Your first stop is **Caldas de Monchique**, a centuries-old spa lying in a lush wooded ravine. Take the second turning on the left, marked with a yellow fountain sign (the first takes you to the bottling plant and thermal hospital), park the car and wander around this faded but still charming spa. People have been coming here since Roman times to take the spring waters of Monchique. The waters (which are meant to do wonders for rheumatism and indigestion) are warm, foul-smelling and spew from a plastic pipe.

Caldas de Monchique

A few drops are said to add years to your life, so give them a try or fill a flagon. You can then return to the square for something that is more likely to stimulate the taste buds: the locally produced *Medronho*. This fiery distilled spirit is made from the berry of the *Arbutus unedo* tree, which grows in profusion around Monchique (you can recognise it by the clusters of white or pink flowers and fleshy strawberry-like berries), and locals say you can only get the real brew in Monchique itself. It is powerful stuff and even a small glass can have an immediate effect on an empty stomach. Try it either at the *bodega* or in the handicrafts centre, which looks a bit like a Moorish palace and used to be a casino. Buy a bottle or two to take back home so you can have a Portuguese party with friends. The **Restaurante Central** (tel: 282-912203) is a pleasantly old-fashioned place reminiscent of Monchique in its heyday, a great spot for lunch. Choose the mountain ham or the chicken *piri-piri*. The alternative to an indoor lunch is a picnic on one of the stone benches beside the cool, babbling brook, which tumbles down the hillside at the far side of the square.

Monchique, tiled bar sign

After lunch leave Caldas (the exit road is via the bottling plant and thermal hospital), turn left and climb up amid forests of eucalyptus, cork, carob and cultivated terraces. When you get to the market town of **Monchique**, follow the signs to the centre and park in the large dusty Largo 5 de Outubro. Take the steep cobbled Rua do Porto Fundo leading up to the centre. The first left takes you up a wide stairway, past the Barlefante (which serves good *tapas* in a cool setting if you still happen

36

Monchique street sign

to be hungry). Turn left further up at the junction where you see a bar advertising 'good port wine', along the rough cobbles and past flaking facades, into the Largo de S Gonçalo de Lagos, then follow the road up into the Caminho do Convento. A short way along, turn left up a pretty wooded track leading to the **convent**, which perches above Monchique among weeds and camellias. The convent is derelict and the only signs of life are a few goats. To gain access, go to the right of the building and walk through to the main chapel. The bell tower offers lovely views of Monchique and a wide sweep of the Serra and coastline. If it is cool and you have the stamina, there is a fine walk from here to the summit of Fóia; you should allow about two hours for the walk to the top and back.

Back on the Caminho do Convento, turn left and zigzag down to the centre, detouring if you wish to explore some of the picturesque side alleys. At the main Rua do Dr Samor Gill turn right past white balconied houses, a picturesque cafe and a tiny church with hand-painted tiles and a carved gilt wooden gallery. Turn left into the Rua da Igreja, passing the **Central Restaurant** whose walls are festooned with euphoric messages from passers-by who have stopped for a drink and stayed for hours (do the same if you wish), then on to the sparkling white **parish church** at the end of the street with its striking Manueline doorway. The interior is beautifully kept, with its coloured tiles, fine wood ceiling, carved side chapels and capitals with intertwined nautical ropes.

Before leaving, look around the town for baskets, handicrafts and large jars of locally made honey, then return to the car, take the road back towards the Caldas but branch off right along the road marked **Fóia**. Wind your way up the mountain to the treeless summit of Fóia at 902 metres (2,960 ft).

Be prepared for cold gusts at the top. You are now at the highest point in the Algarve, so ignore the TV station aerials and tacky stalls and admire the views over the plain to the sea. Optimists say that you can see as far as Sintra, though mists and heat haze often block the best of the views. Early evening (when the tourists have all gone home) is the best time to visit.

En route down the mountain, the **Estalagem Abrigo da Montanha** is a great place to stop for a drink. If you are captivated by the ambience of this mountainside inn, stay for a dinner of *cataplana* and spend the evening far from the madding crowds on the coast.

Monchique church doorway

Morning in the hills of Monchique; mountain drive to Aljezur; evening dip on the west coast.

An excursion into the hills of Monchique could easily occupy a whole day *(see Itinerary 6)*. This rather more ambitious route, dependent on an earlier start, enables you to see Monchique before the morning charabanc of tourists arrives, and to take in the stunning and seldom used route through the mountains west of Monchique to Aljezur and the beaches beyond. It is advisable to pack a sweater for the cool peaks of Monchique. Try to make it to the Caldas de Monchique for breakfast no later than 9.30am.

If you are coming from Portimão, follow signs from the town side of the bridge that guide you onto the N124. The drive takes under half an hour and the route is direct apart from a left turn (well marked) at Porto de Lagos, taking you onto the N266. The terrain changes fairly rapidly, from the parched lands around the coast to the lush foothills of the Serra de Monchique, where luxuriant gardens flourish.

Your first stop is **Caldas de Monchique**, nestling in a verdant ravine and clearly signed to the left off the main road. Breakfast on fresh bread and locally produced honey at the Albergaria Velha in the square. Browse around the spa, walk up by the babbling stream, take the waters and (if it is not too early in the morning) try a nip of Monchique-made Medronho.

By mid morning, leave the Caldas for the market town of **Monchique**, about 7 km (4¼ miles) to the north. On the way you will pass several restaurants specialising in chicken *piri-piri*. Refer again to Itinerary 6 in order to explore the cobbled streets of the town, as well as the routes to the convent and the highest peak in Monchique at Fóia.

By the time you come down the mountain you may well be ready for a midday meal. Take your pick of either **Paraiso da Montanha** (closed Thursday) for mountain ham or chicken piri-piri; or the **Estalagem Abrigo da Montanha** for *cataplana* on the panoramic terrace. It is tempting at either location to while away the afternoon just sipping chilled wine and admiring the views. Do so if you wish but if you are to take in the Atlantic coast today, start off for Aljezur by mid afternoon.

Where the Fóia road meets the main road, turn right towards Portimão, then right again on

Roadside fruit stall

Carrapateira

the road marked to Marmelete (N267). Prepare for a rough but scenic road twisting its way through steep, partially terraced hillsides, with citrus fruit and cork trees. As you proceed, there are good views of the hills beyond the eucalyptus trees. In the sleepy hill village of Marmelete, follow the sign to Aljezur (17 km/11 miles). The road is still marked on maps as a dirt track, which deters all but the most intrepid of travellers. In fact, it is now one of the best roads in the Algarve, with exceptionally little traffic. Cut through red and ochre rocks, barren terrain and wide-open spaces, and then descend towards the coast. This is the best bit, with stunning views down to the coast and rolling, green hills between you and the sea.

The remains of a 10th-century Moorish castle crowning a low hill herald the town of **Aljezur**. The old and new quarters of the town are divided by the rather muddy Aljezur River. Drive through the dull 'new' town (built in the late 18th century as an alternative to the mosquito-infested older quarter) and park just before the bridge, in the square with the tourist office and marketplace. It is possible to drive up to the **Castelo** but the going is steep and the road at the top won't take anything much wider than a small Fiat. Walk across the bridge, turn right through the somewhat dilapidated old Moorish village, and follow signs for the Castelo, up the hill and past the church. Like most castles in the Algarve it was built by the Arabs and destroyed in a series of sieges and earthquakes. Not much remains but there are good views all round. The track descending on the other side brings you to a peaceful local scene of whitewashed cottages with women clad in black typically sitting in doorways, washing flapping in the wind and cats and dogs snoozing in the sun.

From Aljezur you can either head back south (drive over the bridge, turn left for the main N120 to Lagos) or go to the coast for a taste of the real Atlantic. Try either **Arrifana**, 10 km (6 miles) southwest of Aljezur (take the turning to the right 1 km (½ mile) south of the town), or one of the spectacular beaches west of **Carrapateira**. Whichever you choose, watch out for Atlantic rollers and strong currents. Stay around to watch the sun sink from the west coast of Cape St Vincent. The cafe at **Praia do Castelejo** just above the beach is a lovely spot for an early evening meal.

8. Silves – Ancient Capital

Breakfast and sightseeing in Silves, Moorish capital of the Algarve; afternoon on the quiet waters of the Barragem do Arade; sundowner at Algar Seco.

Poets praised its beauty and compared it to Baghdad. Historians described it as more rich and sumptuous than Lisbon. Large vessels made their way up the Arade River from Portimão, loading up with lemons, oranges and cork. Today the citrus trees still flourish (the oranges are said to be the sweetest and juiciest in the Algarve), but **Silves** is a mere shadow of its former self and the river port has long been silted up. What was not destroyed by sieges (most notably the brutal attack by Sancho I and northern crusaders in 1189) fell in the earthquake of 1755. The saving grace is the Moorish fortress, whose battlements still dominate the valley of the River Arade. The massive sandstone walls and turrets crowning the town are a fine sight as you approach from the south or east.

Park if you can on the Praça do Municipio, the square in the centre of town, and take the steep cobbled Rua da Sé up towards the castle. On your right and behind the cathedral you will find the **Café Inglês**, a large 1920s house attractively converted into a cafe/restaurant by its English owners. Stop here for fresh coffee, hot bread made in the hills and homemade marmalade.

Silves' Cathedral

Start your sightseeing at the **Cathedral** (daily 8.30am–1pm and 2.30–6pm). Like the rest of Silves this structure has suffered the ravages of time, but thanks to restoration the impression – at least that of the lofty aisles and naves – is one of pure Gothic. Some of the tombs here are said to be those of crusaders who fell in the final capture of the town. A little way further up you will see the arched gateway of the **Castelo** (open at 9am, entrance free). Within the walls gardens run riot, black cats doze and gipsy-like figures accost you with linen and lace. Nearby stands the larger-than-life statue of Sancho I, 'King of Portugal, Silves and the Algarvians', who laid seige to the Arabs' lavish stronghold. There is a stunning view of the valley of the River Arade and rolling

40

Silves' Castle

hills with rows of orange and lemon trees from the parapets. Directly below are the huge old cisterns and silos where the Moors took refuge before being rooted out and robbed of all their spoils by the crusaders.

Coming back down the Rua da Sé, take the Travessa do Gato to the right, a quiet alley where roosters scratch at the cobbles, canaries pipe and local women gut and wash fish for lunch. Turn left down the steps to the main square, and then take the Rua das Portas de Loulé to reach the excellent Archaeology Museum.

For lunch you could go to the **Fabrica do Inglês** in Rua Gregório Mascareulias (tel: 282-440480). This is a recently converted cork factory, which also houses a museum and is situated just below the castle walls. Alternatively, if you wish to indulge in a feast of shellfish, go to **Rui Marisqueira** (closed Tuesday), across the river at Albergaria Marisqueira. This is one of the best fish restaurants in the Algarve and it is wise to make a reservation before you go (tel: 282-443106).

By late morning set off for the **Barragem do Arade**, a peaceful reservoir 10 km (6 miles) northeast of Silves. Join the main N124 running northeast from the town (signed to São Bartolomeu de Messines), stopping as you come out of town at the 16th-century carved stone cross, the **Cruz de Portugal**, in a pavilion on your left. Here the views of the fortress are particularly fine. Continue on the main road until you see a turning left to the Barragem. Follow the road to a junction, just past a small restaurant, and turn left down a dirt track where figs, oranges and honey are sold by the roadside. Carry on until you come to a restaurant overlooking

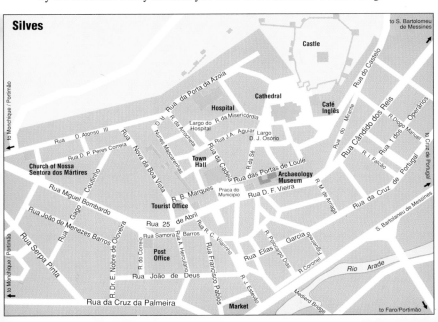

the reservoir. You can rent a motor boat to explore the peaceful waters of the reservoir or take a trip across to the island for swimming, sunbathing or water sports. Even in high season this is a peaceful place, with lovely walks and good picnic spots.

Linger as long as you wish at the reservoir, then head south to Lagoa via Silves. Here you will find the **potteries of Porches** to the east (see *Shopping* section). Porches Pottery (on the right- hand side of the main N125) stays open until 7pm in summer, 6pm in winter. Alternatively, go directly south from Lagoa to Carvoeiro, turn left when you get to the centre of the resort and follow the signs for **Algar Seco**. A flight of steps lead down to this beauty spot of grottoes, arches and pitted ochre rock. The waters here, deep blue and transparent, are a popular haunt of snorkellers. Wrap up the day with a sundowner at the taverna on the rocks after a cooling dip. Afterwards dine at **O Lotus** (tel: 282-352098; closed Sat) in Lagoa (opposite Galp Petrol Station), where local gourmets gather for lobster and exceptional *cataplana* and seafood rice.

9. Albufeira

Braving a day in the Algarve's biggest package resort.

It's the same old saga as the Spanish Costas: a quaint fishing village transformed into a giant cosmopolitan resort. Albufeira is hardly a paradise for the independent traveller, yet sitting as it does in the middle of the Algarve's coast (and providing probably more facilities and hotels than all the resorts to the west of it put together),

Albufeira, Fishermen's Beach

it is hard to ignore. If you do brave a day here, turn a blind eye to the sprawling sky-rise outskirts and make for the winding old alleys and vestigial traces of the fishing village. You may well find that, despite the loud bars and fish-and-chip shops, Albufeira is far prettier than its image might suggest.

Your starting point is the **Largo Cais Herculano**, the old fishermens' quarter behind the **Praia dos Barcos**, or Fishermen's Beach. Lobster pots, piles of nets and painted fishing smacks are all eloquent evidence that, despite the tourist invasion, the fishing industry still survives. If you can stir yourself as early as 7–7.30am you can watch the fishermen unload their catch at the wholesale fish market and the auction nearby at the old fish market. Alternatively, arrive no later than 9–9.30am, before the tourists (who have probably been painting the town red till the early hours of the morning) start to stir. Take continental breakfast at the **Café Oceano,** one of the older fishermen's haunts, which opens early in the morning. Walk inland along the Rua Cândido dos Reis, which was the site of the old fruit market. This takes you northwest up to the **Largo**

Albufeira, the old town

Eng Duarte Pacheco, the main plaza, which has been subject to ruthless modern development. Originally one of the prettier spots in town and the focal point for the open-air market (which used to fill the streets of the centre), it has unfortunately lost a lot of its simple charm in recent years — the chief lure these days is a half-litre of lager at an open-air cafe.

Walk across the square and west into **Rua 5 de Outubro**, the main pedestrianised shopping street of the town, complete with several pavement cafes. Browse around for shoes, ceramics and leisure wear, then come down south towards the sea, past the tourist office and through the tunnel under the Sol y Mar Hotel to see the main **Albufeira beach.** Take a swim here if the water looks inviting and there is room to manoeuvre on the beach, then head back along the Rua 5 de Outubro. About a third of the way along the street, take a left into the Rua da Igreja Nova, past the parish church with its squashed onion domes. At the end of the road cross over the Praça Miguel Bombarda to the domed **Church of São Sebastião** and note the swirling finely carved motifs of the Manueline portal. Turn right and walk along the Rua Latino Coelho for splendid views of the bay. Retrace your steps to the Praça Miguel Bombarda and make a note of the Beach Basket restaurant with sea view terrace — a nice spot for a light lunch later — then go east into the Rua Bernardino de Sousa.

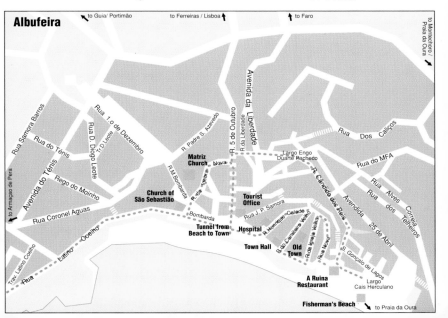

Above and Below: Albufeira beaches

Weave your way through the narrow **alleys of the old town** by turning left into the Rua Henrique Calado. The Chapel of the Misericórdia on the left is a restored 16th-century church possibly built on the site of a Moorish mosque.

At the end of the street turn right into the cobbled Rua do Cemeterio Velho and down to the walled promenade for good views round the bay. Follow the promenade a short way east, then turn left up the peaceful Rua da Igreja Velha, take a right at the top and go down the cobbled Rua Nova. **Mor's Country Kitchen** (advertising 'English Bif, 25 miles sea view and best looking staff') is at the end of the street. The restaurant/bar **A Ruina** perches precariously on the cliff with a roof-top bar and several levels where, when it's time for lunch, you can eat fish fresh from the market and look down on the bay. Prices here are on the steep side and service in high season has a tendency to be brusque, but because of its dramatic location the establishment continues to pull in the crowds.

Alternatively, you could head back to the Beach Basket restaurant in Praça Miguel Bombarda or try one of the many cheaper tavernas in town and enjoy a traditional Portuguese meal of a plate of sardines, salad and a jug of wine.

If your afternoon priority is a beach, you can try either the **Olhos de Agua** to the east of Albufeira, or **São Rafael**, **Castelo** or **Galé** to the west, all less crowded than Albufeira, but by no means undiscovered. If this does not appeal to you, and you want to escape from the crowds on firm land, you can take boat trips from Praia da Oura (2 km east of Albuteira). For information, telephone 289-586160 or 917-637313. This should cost between 2,000$00 and 7,500$00.

44

10. Hill Village Tour from Albufeira

Morning in the hill villages of Alte and Salir; lunch at Querença; afternoon shopping/sightseeing in Loulé.

Alte is arguably the prettiest of all the hill villages, more by virtue of its well-kept, whitewashed houses, clean cobbled streets and lush gardens than any architectural merit. The area is delightful for walks and picnics in the hills. Avoid visiting on Saturday afternoons in season, when a deluge of tourists may descend on the village. If you are lucky, your visit may coincide with the monthly market.

If you are coming from Albufeira, you could make a brief diversion to the village of Paderne for its Manueline church and castle ruins; and/or to **São Bartolomeu** de Messines, 12 km (7½ miles) to the northwest to see another example of the Manueline in the curious red sandstone church with its twisted stone columns.

The village of Alte

At **Alte**, park at the Fonte Pequena (Little Fountain) beside the mountain stream and walk to the centre, passing pristine patios, balconies brimming with plants and brilliant splashes of colour from hibiscus, oleander and geraniums. The church is filled with flowers and is embellished with blue-and-white glazed tiles and colourful religious statuary.

If the church is shut, a key can be obtained from the lady who lives in the first house (red door) of Rua Dr Manuel Figueiredo. Take the steps to your left as you face the church door, and the street is the first one on the left. There are several cafes lying in the shadow of the church, if you feel the need for refreshment. Portuguese tend to patronise the **Altense** just below the entrance where, morning dews or rain-showers permitting, you can join them for a saucer of snails (*caracóis*) and Sagres beer. At the other end of the village, on your way back to the Fonte Pequena, there is a baroque chapel on the small square and an adjoining museum with an idiosyncratic collection of metal pots, rat traps, cow bells and 1930s' photos of the Alte Village band.

On a scorching hot day you may want to cool off at the **Fonte Grande** (beyond Fonte Pequena) where there is a waterfall of sorts and stone benches in the shade of trees. Alte is famed for the purity of its spring and people used to come for miles around to collect the waters.

Take the main N124 going east out of the village and drive on for about

45

12 km (7½ miles) through unspoilt rural scenery until you come to **Salir** on your right. Another 'hill village', this one is not so orderly as Alte, but has the distinct advantage of being off the tourist itineraries. Follow the signs to the **Castelo**, which, as you will see, is now no more than chunks of old Arab fortress walls integrated with village houses. You can park near the tiny bar and wander round this little oasis where patios overflow with plants, geraniums tumble over stone walls and dogs nap peacefully in the sunshine.

From here you can look across to the centre of Salir where the church dominates and the houses are jumbled on the hillside below. Have a look around, then return to the road you came in on and follow it southward (towards Loulé) through the hills and past villages too tiny to be marked on maps.

At Ponte de Tor (7 km/4¼ miles) turn left for **Querença** and continue for about 4 km until you see a small road to the right marked to the village. You come into the village square where the pretty baroque church of Nossa Senhora do Pé

da Cruz is set against a background of green hills. If it is open, the *azelejos* inside are worth a look. Take the road at the far side of the square, then proceed a little further: on your left, you will

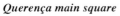

Querença main square

see the entrance to the **Quinta do Olival** restaurant (tel: 289-422969). Stop here for lunch, preferably on the panoramic terrace which surveys a huge sweep of hills to the south. Local specialities are served, including the perennial favourite, almond cake.

Your afternoon destination is **Loulé**. Turn left out of the restaurant, and follow the signposts for Loulé, taking the N396 south through hilly terrain forested with pine, eucalyptus and cork. At Loulé, turn left at the major crossroads, then left again at the roundabout, and park your car on the main tree lined boulevard. *See Itinerary 11* and spend your afternoon in the town shopping for local handicrafts and souvenirs, sightseeing or just wandering at your leisure.

11. Lunch in Loulé

Market town of Loulé: sights, shops and market stalls. To see Loulé at its liveliest go on a Saturday morning when the main market is in full swing.

If your starting point is Faro, make a brief diversion to take in the **Igreja de São Lourenço**, a gem of a church set on a hillock above the N125, east of Almansil. To get there, go about 2.5 km (1½ miles) beyond the turn-off to Loulé, take the narrow turning to the right marked to São Lourenço and you will come up to the church. The frenzy of the N125 contrasts sharply with this quiet oasis, where cool blue-and-white tiles embellish every inch of walls and vaulting, setting off the sumptuous gilded altar. Leaving the church (and a few *escudos* for the upkeep), turn right onto the N125, right again at Almansil and follow the signs to the town of Loulé. When you arrive there (7 km/4¼ miles from Almansil), ignore the outlying modern sprawl and head for the centre, parking if you can on the wide tree lined boulevard, Avenida José da Costa Mealha.

The **market** is a good place to start, an unmistakable mock-Moorish structure with pink onion-shaped domes. On a Saturday surrounding streets will be packed with shoppers browsing through the stalls selling local produce: buckets of black and green olives, baskets of beans, sacks of almonds, strings of sausages, boxes of

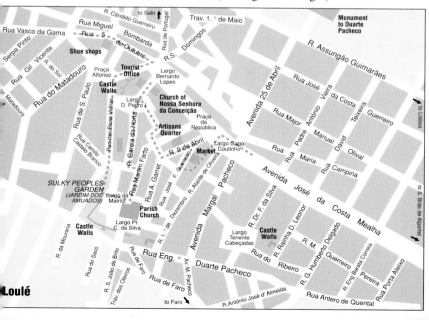

Loulé

oranges and bunches of coriander. Take your pick of the produce, then make your way inside the covered market (a daily feature) where baby chicks and ducklings are sold in shoe boxes and local black-clad peasants squat alongside the walls with a basket of eggs or a pair of rabbits huddled in a box. On the far side, stalls sell chunky earthenware plates, pots and vases at excellent prices.

Leave the market on this side and turn right along the Rua José F Guerreiro, then sharp left down the cobbled **Rua 9 de Abril**. Listen for the sound of hammers and sanders and peek into the narrow doorways of workshops where local artisans are making copper and brass pots and pans. Turn right at the crossroads, past the Free Times Bar, and follow the road right down to the tourist office, passing en route the law courts and a convent converted into a stylish modern art gallery. The tourist office, where you can pick up leaflets on Loulé and sur-

rounds, lies across the Rua D Paio Peres Correia. Above it, you can enjoy views of the local area from the recently restored castle walls and visit the Municipal Museum.

Coming out of the courtyard turn left and across the road for the inconspicuous-looking **Church of Nossa Senhora da Conceição**. If it's locked get the key from the frail old lady at No 27 opposite, encouraging her with a few *escudos*. The key opens the brown painted door to the left of the church. Walk through a tiny makeshift chapel and enter the church through the entrance on the right. The interior is a delightful combination of gilded carving and blue and white *azulejos* depicting biblical scenes. Retrace your steps, pass the tourist office, then diagonally cross the Largo D Pedro I into Rua Garcia da Horta, a cobbled alley of pretty houses; turn left at the top, then right into Rua Martim Farto. From here you'll see the lofty bell tower of the **parish church**. Walk up to the square, and into the church, entering through the carved portal. Note inside the finely tiled panels, Manueline carving and curious capitals. If the church is closed, try to get the key from the priest who lives at 19 Calçada dos Sapateiros, the street at the right hand corner of the square if you are standing with your back to the church.

After leaving the church, relax under the shady palms in the gardens opposite (closed at lunch) and try to work out why they are called the *Jardin dos Amuados*, or Sulky People's Garden. Turn down the Calçada dos Sapateiros *(see above)*, then

Opposite and Below: Loulé's market

down the steps to the left which bring you into the Rua Martim Moniz. Turn right here and see the startling contrast of old and modern Loulé. There is a pottery workshop on your right at Nos. 43–5 (if open) and the Restaurante Bica Velha at Nos. 17–19, which is said to occupy the oldest building in town. Have a look at the menu in case you want to return for lunch (good bets are prawns in hot sauce and grey mullet with fennel and *Medronho*).

Carry on down the road until you come to the square, Praça Afonso III, and turn right into the Rua da Barbaça where there are more artisans and the shops are full of their handicrafts. Turn left into the Rua 5 de Outubro, a pedestrianised street which contains shoe shops and several open-air cafes.

Lunch either at the **Bica Velha** or for something with a bit more Portuguese ambience try **Avenida Velha** (closed on Sunday) which is situated above the Shell petrol station on the Avenida José Costa Mealha. Here sardines, sausage, salad and olives are included in the price, so there's no need to order a starter unless of course you are ravenously hungry. If it is not a Saturday (when shops close at 1pm) or Sunday, you can spend any spare time in the afternoon browsing around for leather goods (particularly shoes), ironwork, copper, brass and palm, cane and wickerwork.

Faro, old harbour

12. Faro – Capital City

Morning in Faro, strolling around the harbour and historic city; shopping and lunch; optional trip to Praia de Faro.

Faro's international airport opened in 1965 and since then tourists have been pouring in to a vastly extended airport terminal. Many see no more than the view from the skies: a large, concrete sprawl, separated from the ocean by long thin sand spits and a series of islets. Admittedly, Faro's architectural make-up has been severely impoverished by sieges, raids and earthquakes, but to ignore the inner city, where relics of the old walls and traces of Gothic and much of the baroque survive, is to miss one of the finest old quarters of the Algarve. If you visit in high season, arrive early to avoid parking problems. Bear in mind too that the cathedral closes at noon and most sites are shut at weekends. Park close to the waterfront and start the day with a stroll around the palm-lined harbour. Stop for coffee/breakfast in the harbourside gardens or in the brasserie-styled **Café Aliança** across the road in Rua Dr Francisco Gomes.

The inner or historic centre lies to the south. The approach is through the **Arco da Vila**, a handsome Italianate arch flanked by two Ionian columns and topped by a belfry whose high vantage point provides a home for nesting storks. The figure in the niche above the arch is St Thomas Aquinas, who was made patron saint of the city for saving it from the plague in the early 17th century.

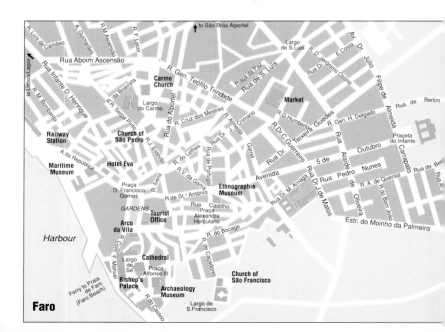

Arco da Vila

The cobbled, whitewashed Rua do Municipo leads up from the archway to the **Largo da Sé,** Largo being the cobbled square and *Sé* the omnipresent cathedral (open 10am–noon, Sunday 8am–1pm). Note the old Bishop's Palace to your right, the Town Hall to your immediate left and then enter the heavy Gothic portal on the west side of the cathedral. Gone is most of the Gothic influence, but there are some fine 18th-century glazed tiles in the side chapels, notably in the second chapel on the left and the last chapels either side of the naves.

Coming out of the cathedral turn left and explore the quiet primitive quarter in and around the cobbled Rua do Arco. Turn along the Rua Professor Norberto da Silva, where pots of plants hang on faded facades and the only sounds are canaries trilling in their cages. Pass the Taverna da Sé on your right and come into the **Praça Afonso III,** dominated by a statue of the determined-looking Dom Afonso III (1210–79), who effectively put an end to Moorish hegemony in the Algarve. No. 14 at the bottom of the square on your right is the **Archaeological Museum** (Monday–Saturday 9.30am–noon and 2–5pm, entrance 150$). The exhibits have an exceptionally beautiful setting in the quiet cloistered galleries of a restored renaissance convent. Upper galleries (paintings, pottery, silver and furniture) are unlikely to inspire but there are good views of the gargoyles on the cloisters.

Before you leave the old centre note the menu at the **Cidade Velha** on the east side of the Largo da Sé, the only restaurant in the historic city, which also happens to be one of the best (and most expensive) in Faro. Typical dishes are fresh clams with garlic and coriander, succulent prawns in chilli sauce and fillet of pork with dates, walnuts and port. If this whets the appetite, book a table for lunch later on.

Leave the old city via the Arco de Repousa off the Praça Afonso III. The arch is best viewed from the far side. Turn right into the large desolate Largo de São Francisco and make for the church beside the barracks (the Faro Infantry occupy the adjoining monastery.) If the church is closed, ring the bell on the door to the left of the entrance. With luck it should open automatically.

Cross the pretty courtyard and enter the church by the door on the right. A modest facade belies an internal extravaganza of blue and gold, created by the sumptuous gilded and lacquered wood-carvings and the glazed tiles with scenes from the life of

Feeding pigeons in the harbour-side gardens

St Francis. Leaving the church, turn right into the Rua de Caçadores and carry on to the Praça Alexandre Herculano. The Casa de Lumena (an above average pensão) used to belong to one of Faro's fishing magnates. Continue till you come to the Praça da Liberdade. On the corner to your right is a large building containing the **Ethnographic Museum** (9.30am–noon and 2–5.30pm weekdays, entrance 250$), depicting traditional Algarvian life: tuna nets, lobster pots, baskets, beehives, a replica of a peasant house and a typical coloured fishing smack with a painted eye to ward off the devil.

Exiting the museum, take a left turn off the square into the pedestrianised **Rua de Santo António**. This is the main shopping street in Faro. Stop for a drink in an open-air cafe, then spend what remains of the morning singling out the best shops (Oberon at No. 67, first shop on your right, is very tempting for leather).

Shops shut at 1pm at which point you can either return to the Cidade Velha *(see above)* or choose a restaurant closer by. At the end of Rua Santo António, take a right turn up to the Praça Ferreira de Almeida; this is the place for fish restaurants. Two to try are **Dois Irmãos** (specialising in Cataplana, *see page 86*) and the **Sol e Jardim** next door.

After lunch but not before 3pm, take the Rua José Estevão northwest from the Praça Ferreira de Almeida. Pass the church of São Pedro on your right and, further on, come into the Largo do Carmo, with its unmistakable

São Francisco church

twin-belfried baroque **Church of Carmo** standing somewhat incongrously among modern high-rise blocks (open Monday to Saturday 10am–1pm and 3–5pm, Sunday during services). The interior is embellished with lavish woodcarvings, but far more striking is the macabre **Capela dos Ossos** (Chapel of Bones). Ask the sacristan and you will be taken to this tiny chapel hidden in the cemetery at the back of the church. Prepare to face the chilling bones and grinning skulls of 1,254 monks and parishioners covering the walls.

Make your way back to the harbour and pay a brief visit to the **Maritime Museum** in the Harbour Master's building, northwest of the harbour. The **Praia de Faro** is nearby, not one of the loveliest Algarve beaches but good enough to tempt you in for a dip. Buses go from the harbour gardens. To get there by car, *Praia de Faro* is signed to the right when you're in sight of the radar tower. Alternatively, take a ferry to the Ilha da Culatra. Ask at the tourist office near the Arco da Vila, for times.

13. Cultural Core – Faro to Olhão

Morning sightseeing/shopping in Faro; leisurely lunch, Roman ruins and rococo Palace in Estói; village of Moncarapacho and views from Serra de San Miguel; a fish dinner in Olhão.

This is a short tour (30 km/18¾ miles), but one which covers several high spots of the eastern half of the Algarve, both cultural and geographical. Avoid visiting on Sunday and Monday, when sites are closed, but if you happen to be anywhere near Estói on the second Sunday of the month, don't miss the 'gipsy' market.

Antique shop

Park as close to Faro harbour as you can and spend the morning sightseeing. Cover as many sites from Itinerary 12 as you wish, but make the **Centro Histórico** your top priority and bear in mind that the cathedral closes at noon. By late morning leave behind the hubbub and heat of the city and head for the quiet countryside north of Faro. The simplest way of getting to **Estói** (pronounced Shtoe-ee) is to head west from the harbour, following the signs for Faro airport and Portimão, then turn right when you see the signs for São Brás de Alportel. This will bring you onto the N2, where the sprawling suburbs of Faro gradually give way to groves of orange and lemon trees. Carry on until you see a fork right from Estói (you are now roughly 11 km/7 miles from Faro), followed by another right turn. The Ruínas de Milreu (Roman ruins) are on your left before the village – you will return here later on this itinerary.

For lunch, choose between two extremes. Either join the locals in the cheap **Café Retiro dos Arcos** (inconspicuously signed on the left shortly before the church) for generous helpings of charcoal-grilled chicken or chops, or treat yourself to the more hedonistic pleasures of **Monte do Casal** (tel: 289-991503), where you can indulge in smoked potted quail mousse and salmon trout by the pool or in the converted coach house.

This country house restaurant is set in lovely gardens 3 km (1¾ miles) from Estói with views south to the sea. To get there follow the yellow signs from the centre of Estói. The place is not very Portuguese (English run with a chef who trained with the London based Savoy group of hotels), but it's an ideal spot to unwind after the frenzy of Faro.

The sleepy village of Estói gives you no clue that it is the setting

Moncarapacho museum

of the most lavish manor house in Algarve. **The Palace of the Counts of Estói** (Tuesday–Sunday 10am–12.30pm and 2–5pm; admission free) lies behind high stone walls close to the village centre. As you face the steps of the church, take the road to your left which leads down to the palace gates. An alley of palm trees leads to the terraces and gardens of this rococo palace. Constructed in the 18th century and added to in a variety of styles since that time, it is an intriguing (if not aesthetically satisfying) faded pink villa. The house continues to undergo sporadic restoration, and remains closed to the public. You can, however, stroll around the fantasy garden, full of fountains, balustraded terraces, neoclassical statues and sweet smelling flowerbeds. Note the fine tiled panels along the stone stairways, the semi-clothed statues, the busts of notables and – hidden below the main balustrade – a replica of Canova's *Three Graces*.

Return to the ruins of **Milreu** (open Tuesday–Sunday, 10am–12.30pm and 2–5pm) and park the car by the gates. Although they appear somewhat scant and overgrown from the roadside, these Roman

remains deserve a good half hour, if only for the mosaics. The ruins were first excavated in 1877, and date from the 2nd–6th centuries. You can still see some fragments of capitals, relics of kitchens and baths from the original Roman villa, but the richest spoils (statues, imperial busts, ceramics, gravestones and mosaics) were taken and then distributed among museums in Portugal (Faro Archaeological and Lagos Regional Museums, among them) and various private collections.

To locate mosaics of fish and crustaceans consult the map in English on the site. The big solid water sanctuary, which rises above the ruins on the south side, looks more like a Gallic/Roman temple and was, in fact, used as a church when the Visigoths took over the region.

Leave Estói on the Olhão road, then take the turning left to Moncarapacho (passing the Monte do Casal). After around 8 km (5 miles), cross the main N398 and take the road into the centre of Moncarapacho. Park in the main square and amble around this quiet and simple Algarve village. At siesta time dogs will be dozing in the shade of the church, old men drinking in *tasca* bars and young ones glued to TV soaps in the local cafe. The finest example of architecture in the village is the carved Renaissance portal of the parish church in the square.

The hours of the nearby chapel and adjoining museum are restricted to 11am–3pm Monday, Wednesday and Friday, but you might want to try your powers of persuasion and ask the local priest who lives opposite the main church to show you round the idiosyncratic collection of archaeological finds and sacred art.

The back streets of Olhão

The **chapel of Santo Cristo**, next door, traditionally famed as a place of miracles, is covered with handsome *azulejos* in yellow, blue and white.

As evening approaches, return to the N398, turn right and take the first left, a narrow road marked inconspicuously Serra de San Miguel. If it is cool and an 8-km (5-mile) hike up the hillside does not daunt you, proceed by foot and enjoy the scenery. The road winds up through lemon and orange groves, carobs and figs, then opens out onto red rocky slopes of macchia and wild flowers. For centuries this mountain was considered sacred and pilgrims would come here to seek spiritual solace or to rub themselves in its supposedly therapeutic earth. Today it is still a beauty spot,

though somewhat marred by the radio station that sits at the top.

Afterwards, return to the main N398 and turn right for Olhão. When you get to the town, follow the signs for the **Mercados**, driving past the fishing port, and park on the main Avenida 5 de Outubro close to the covered marketplace. It is well worth taking the time to explore the fascinating old winding alleys of the fishermens' quarter.

As evening falls and the aroma of fresh fish sizzling on charcoal starts to stimulate your digestive juices, return to the Avenida 5 de Outubro. There are a range of restaurants here, so you can afford to be choosy. Once you have decided, relax and order whatever variety of fish takes your fancy from the menu.

14. Off the Beaten Track – São Bras to Tavira

Breakfast at São Brás de Alportel, spectacular mountain drive up to Cachopo and down to Tavira.

This 70 km (43½ mile) tour through remote mountains is particularly pretty in spring when the slopes are dotted with white rock rose blossoms. On a really hot day the trip is best left until late afternoon or early evening when the sun silhouettes the hills and mountains.

For a morning tour, begin the day at the Pousada at São Brás de Alportel. Equivalent to the Spanish *paradores*, the Portuguese *pousadas* are state run, off the beaten track and usually offer good views. The Pousada at São Brás is no exception, sitting on a hill and surveying a wide sweep of the eastern Algarve. To get there take the main N2 Lisbon road north from the town of São Brás. After approximately 2 km (1¼ miles) take the right turn marked to the Pousada, along a drive of fig trees. Breakfast, at 1,200$, is no giveaway, but by Algarvian standards it is exceptionally good and you can help yourself to as much as you like and enjoy the views at the same time.

Return to the Lisbon road and head north through eucalyptus trees and cork oaks. Just after Barranco do Velho (13 km/8 miles), take the road marked to Cachopo. You'll now be travelling through a very remote hilly region of the Algarve, far removed from the hubbub of the coast. Spring is the prettiest time, when the slopes are deep green, and the cistus and broom are in flower, but the

pine trees and the tall eucalyptus add interest to the hillsides all year round.

Stop for a drink at **Cachopo**, a simple village with a couple of bars and café-restaurants serving seafood. From here you can either take an extended scenic route, north to Alcoutim and then south along the River Guadiana, or take the N397 to Tavira, which snakes down through a spectacular landscape of rolling hills. The journey is less than 40 km (25 miles) but the winding road and rough patches make it feel a lot longer. There are some lovely views if you dare take your eyes off the twisting road. You won't see much civilisation here – just the odd donkey cart laden with grass, brown and white speckled goats grazing on the hillside and the occasional white farmhouse nestling in a valley. It is worth allowing an hour or two to explore the elegant centre of Tavira. Itinerary 17 covers the main points of interest here and makes several suggestions for lunch.

15. The Sotavento – Olhão and Tavira

Fish market in Olhão; lunch in Tavira; swim at Monte Gordo; castle at Castro Marim.

What the Sotavento lacks in dramatic coastal scenery – saltpans, sand bars and citrus fruits – is to a large degree compensated for by the refreshing absence of package-style holiday resorts and the fact that it has two of the most interesting places to visit along the entire Algarve coast: Olhão and Tavira. The word 'Sotavento' means leeward and the coast along here is partially protected by a shoreline of sand pits. Arrive in **Olhão** as early as you can to see the fish market in full swing *(see Itinerary 16, page 61)*. Take plenty of film and a flash gun to snap the fishwives laying out the purchases

in big flat baskets, and record the sheer variety of fish and seafood piled up high on the stalls. Spend an hour exploring the alleys of the fishermens' quarter and view the flat-roofed houses and forest of chimneys and aerials from the belfry of the parish church.

By mid morning take the N125, following the signs for Vila Real and head for Tavira (22 km/13¾ miles). The road is first-class for the Algarve but the scenery is uninspiring, with straggling development and real estate ads interspersed among the wayside carob and lemon trees. As you get to the centre of Luz de Tavira, on your left is the doorway of the parish church, a fine example of Manueline

Castro Marim

architecture. Further on, look out for wayside *artesanato* stalls – a good source for *cataplanas*, liquor stills, rugs and basketry. Take the turning off to **Tavira** and, as you come towards the centre, follow the signs to Vila Real, which will bring you to the main **Praça da República**. Park here if you can. From here you are a stone's throw from all the key features of the city: the old stone bridge, the riverside gardens with their stately palms, the marketplace, the castle and the two main churches. Begin with a drink in one of the open-air cafes, then consult Itinerary 17, which details the main attractions of the town, and spend the rest of the morning sightseeing, shopping or taking a pedalo along the river. Before you move on, have lunch at one of the recommended restaurants.

From Tavira take the road to Vila Real (23 km/14¼ miles), past lush farmlands of figs, carob and citrus fruits. Side roads lead off to beaches, but **Monte Gordo**, 3 km (1¾ miles) before Vila Real, is the best place for a swim. The waters here are the warmest along the coast, so take a dip or hire a wind-surfer if time permits.

Leave for **Castro Marim** at the latest by 4pm. If you want to go in style ask at the tourist office (east of the casino on the beach) if the horsedrawn carriages are running. By car you return to the N125, turn right, follow the road for nearly 3 km (1¾ miles) and take the left turn marked Beja, Lisbon and Castro Marim. Drive through the region's nature reserve, slow down to spot waders in the lagoons, then head towards the mighty ruins of the 13th-century fortress of **Castro Marim**. The battlements offer a 360-degree panorama of the area and a bird's eye view of Spain. Head back from here or end the day with a drink at one of the cafes in the stately square of **Vila Real de Santo António**.

Portuguese Water Dogs (*lão d'água*)

The curly-haired Portuguese water dog has been assisting the fishermen of Algarve for centuries. It formed part of the crew of caravels and galleons and is known to have saved sailors and fishermen from drowning in high seas. It loves to swim and dive and has membranes on its paws. It plunges deep, guides fish into nets and can catch them between its teeth.

With the changes in fishing traditions in the 1950s and 1960s this extraordinary breed was in real danger of extinction. But there are still said to be about 1,000 thorough-breds in the country. Half a dozen of them are kept in captivity in the Ria Formosa Nature Reserve near Olhão. They are extremely congenial creatures, more like large curly-haired mongrels than poodles. If you want to have a look, ask for directions from the tourist office in Olhão (Rua do Comércio), then ask at the nature reserve for permission to view them.

Olhão

16. Port of Olhão

A day in and around the port of Olhão; fish and food markets; the fishermen's quarters, fish lunch; by ferry to the offshore islands.

In 1808, 17 intrepid fishermen took a small boat all the way to Rio de Janeiro to tell the exiled Portuguese King, João VI, that Napoleon's troops had left his kingdom. As a reward, the village on the sands was raised to the status of a town and titled Olhão da Restauração. The fishing industry expanded rapidly, canneries were created and, by the mid 19th century, Olhão had become a prosperous port. Fish markets, fishermen's quarters and nudist beaches are not everyone's cup of tea, and the average Algarve package tourist has probably never heard of Olhão. However, for the independent traveller, this has to be one of the most underrated places in the Algarve.

Make an early start to see the pick of the morning catch before it is whisked off by the local restaurateurs (the lobsters will have gone already). When you reach the town, follow the signs for **Porto de Pesca/Mercados**, which take you down the broad Avenida 5 de Outubro. Stop at the ferry terminal to enquire about the departure times of boats going to the islands in the afternoon. Then stroll through the well-nurtured **Patrão Joaquim Lopes gardens,** beside palms, flowerbeds and a carp pond with ducks and terrapins. The covered **markets** lie beyond, two distinctive redbrick turreted buildings, one for fruit and vegetables, the other devoted to fish and seafood. Start with the fish market (the far building) and spend as long as you like looking at the amazing variety of seafood: sea bass and sea bream, crab claws and crayfish, whole conger eel, huge chunks of tuna, heaps of gleaming sardines, writhing inky squid, starfish and spider crabs and live cockles twitching in trays of water.

Exit the market on the waterfront side where coloured smacks are moored and fish hang drying like coat hangers. Nip into the neighbouring food market for oranges, dates or apricots; then stroll around

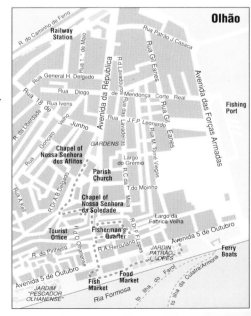

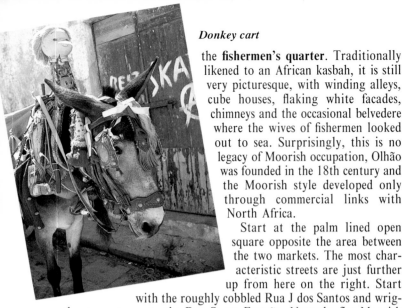

Donkey cart

the **fishermen's quarter**. Traditionally likened to an African kasbah, it is still very picturesque, with winding alleys, cube houses, flaking white facades, chimneys and the occasional belvedere where the wives of fishermen looked out to sea. Surprisingly, this is no legacy of Moorish occupation, Olhão was founded in the 18th century and the Moorish style developed only through commercial links with North Africa.

Start at the palm lined open square opposite the area between the two markets. The most characteristic streets are just further up from here on the right. Start with the roughly cobbled Rua J dos Santos and wriggle your way up to the Rua Santo Estevão. Note the flat Moorish architecture, tiled facades, 'claw' door knockers and washing hanging on street corners. In the Rua Santo Estevão, at No. 31, beside his cobbler's shop, **Mário Caleça** may be playing *fado* on his Portuguese guitar. Pause at the doorway and he may suggest some Frank Sinatra (or more *fado* if you prefer).

Turn right at the end of the street, then take your first left into the Rua do Comércio, a pedestrian shopping street with attractive patterned paving and facades above modern shop fronts. Admire them before they come under the demolition order. Some are already being torn down to give way to drab modern styles. Turn left down the Rua da Soledade into a small square overlooked by a white baroque chapel. The main **parish church** is in the next street on the right. Go inside and ask at the sacristy (top left-hand corner)

Drying fish in Olhão

Olhão rooftops

for access to the belfry. At the top there are good views of the flat-topped roofs, chimneys, terraces and TV aerials of the old quarter. Try to avoid a visit on the hour or the vibrations of the deafening old church bell may shatter your eardrums.

Exit the church and go to the rear of the building (facing the Avenida da República). Here you will see women praying at a little chapel where candles burn among wax *ex votos* of human legs, arms and faces. This is the **Chapel of Nossa Senhora dos Aflitos**. Here fishermen's wives have traditionally come to pray for the safety of their menfolk when there are storms at sea.

Return to the Avenida 5 de Outubro and choose one of the fish restaurants for lunch. You are unlikely to be disappointed whether you opt for live lobsters, swordfish, bream or bass or a simple plate of sardines. For the latter try **O Boté**, beyond the fish market on the right, one of several cafe-like haunts of the locals where you can tuck into as many grilled sardines as you like, with salad, for a few hundred escudos, all washed down with tumblers full of refreshing *vinho da casa*.

After lunch explore the tiny streets of yet another fishermens' quarter, this one even more African-looking and fascinating than the quarter seen this morning. A relaxing afternoon can be spent simply sitting and watching the fishermen sitting on makeshift stools in the street, mending lobster pots and knotting hooks to long lines. Women will probably be slicing or washing fish, or fanning a few sardines grilling on hot coals. To get into the heart of this ethnic quarter take the Rua de Barreta off the Avenida 5 de Outubro (almost opposite the bandstand in the gardens) and work your way east.

Spend the rest of the day on one of Olhão's pair of offshore islands. Both are serviced by ferries and feature sandy beaches but, for preference, opt for the **Ilha da Armona**. The trip across to this long, skinny sand spit takes about 15 minutes. When you get to the island, walk for about a kilometre (½ mile) to the far side in order to reach the unspoilt beaches and sand dunes. Strip off (literally if you like) and spend the afternoon swimming in the warm sea and soaking up the sun.

Sightseeing in the town of Tavira; Cataplana lunch; optional foray into the interior or afternoon on the beach.

Straddling the broad River Gilão and filled with fine old houses and over 30 churches, **Tavira** retains an elegance that most towns in the Algarve have lost. Holidaymakers based west of Faro rarely bother to pay it a visit and despite the new international bridge across the River Guadiana and the motorway link with Spain, the town and surroundings remain relatively uncommercialised.

Arrive no later than 10am to secure a parking space in the main square, **Praça da República**. From here wander through the riverside **gardens**, where stately palms sway gently in the breeze, and admire the view from the riverside. Upstream is a stone arched bridge whose foundations go back to Roman times. Walk to the far end of the gardens, through the green wrought-iron gates of the market and take your pick of figs, almonds and other fruits from the Sotavento's lush farmlands, freshly delivered to the market stall every day. The morning's fish catch will be displayed at the far end of the market. Not so long ago, Tavira was a major port for tuna fishing, the starting point for bloody battles waged between the tuna and the fishermen, which are sometimes described as the 'bullfights of the sea'.

Return to the Praça da República (stopping if you wish at one of the open-air cafes by the gardens for coffee), where you will find the tourist office up the cobbled steps opposite up the town hall. On the way up is the Renaissance portal of the **Church of Misericórdia** (if it is open, which normally it is not, go inside to see the gilded woodwork and *azulejos*); turn left up towards the **Church of Santa Maria do Castelo**, built on the site of a former mosque. If closed, try the door of the sacristan at No. 50 Calçada de D Ana (the road to the right and parallel as you look at the belfry). The chancel houses the tomb of Dom Paio Peres Correia, who liberated large chunks of the Algarve from the Moors), and an inscription

Tavira

Tavira — map

to Vila Real de Santo António · R. dos Fumeiros de Traz · Church of Carmo · Largo do Carmo · Rua do Salto · Pr. 5 de Outubro · Rio Séqua · R. J. Vaz Corte Real · R. de A. Botelho · R. Almirante Cândido dos Reis · O Pátio Restaurant · R. A. Cabreira · Rua J. Joaquim Jara · Rua dos Pelames · Bridge · Rua Jaques Pessoa · Rio Gilão · Chapel of São Brás · Praça da República · Rua do · Rua GARDENS Cais · Market · Church of Misericórdia · J. Pires Padinha · Santa Maria do Castelo · Castle · Tourist Office · Canecão Restaurant · Church of Santiago · Rua da Liberdade · R. D. M. Franco · R. 1. de Maio · to Ilha ou Praia de Tavira · Rua dos Mouros · R. Dr. A. Carlos · R. Dr. S. Falcão · Rua Guilherme · G. Fernandes · Rua Montalvão · Rua Dr. Miguel Bombarda · R. Terente Couto · Rua 25 de Abril · Rua das Freiras · to Faro/ S. Brás de Alportel · Rua Dr. M. Teixeira de Azevedo · Praça Z Guerreiro · São Francisco Monastery · Rua Poeta · Campo dos Mártires da Pátria · Av. Dr. M. Teixeira · Barracks

---

commemorating the seven Christian knights who, during a truce, were killed by Moors while out on a hunting expedition near Tavira.

The walls are the only remaining part of the castle. However, from the gardens inside them, there are some good views of the town's rooftops and church domes.

Make your way back to the central square and cross over the bridge, noting the plaque on this side commemorating the bravery of the locals when they repelled the invading troops of King Juan I of Castile in 1383–5. On the left bank of the river there is a stunning vista which takes in church spires, tiled roofs and castle ramparts. Wander at leisure on this side of the river, starting with the Rua Dr António Cabreira to peek into artisans' workshops and an intriguing antique/bric-a-brac shop on the left as you go down. On the opposite side of the road is the O Pátio restaurant, a possibility for lunch later on (see below). You can spend what remains of the morning nosing around the back streets, *tasca* bars and boutiques of the west bank. For lunch try one of the local *cataplanas* — a soup-cum-casserole served in a special domed tin or copper vessel. Supplies of fish permitting, you have the choice of lobster *cataplana* at **O Pátio**, clams *cataplana* at the **Imperial**, facing the public gardens (not as grand as it sounds) or the slightly cheaper **O Canecão** further along the same road, past the market, which also serves clams with rabbit (in season) and excellent fish soup and seafood rice. Tavira is traditionally a tuna fishing port and you won't have to go very far to find a fresh tuna steak. If you are feeling brave, ask for a glass or two of heady Tavira wine to go with it.

With time in the afternoon, you may choose to follow Itinerary 14 up to Cachopo through lovely hill scenery or (if it is too hot for touring) join the sun seekers on the **Ilha da Tavira**, a sand spit lying offshore and reached by ferry from Tavira beach. The terminal, served by buses in the summer months, is 2 km (1¼ miles) from the centre of town, past the marketplace and through the saltpans.

Vila Real de Santo António

18. Borderlines

Half-day visit to the border towns of Vila Real de Santo António and Ayamonte in Spain.

For a real taste of Spain you need to go as far as Seville. **Ayamonte**, an ordinary border town, can't compare with the famous cities of Andalusia, but the ferry trip is quite fun and very cheap. There is no need to change your money into Spanish pesetas – escudos, pounds, dollars – anything seems to go these days here. A bridge now spans the River Guadiana and links Spain with Portugal, but the ferry service continues to operate. Allow half an hour or more for **Vila Real de Santo António**, a town submerged by the sea in the 17th century, then rebuilt in 1774 in a matter of months. The mastermind behind the speedy reconstruction was the Marquês de Pombal, Chief Minister to King José I, who had already raised parts of Lisbon from their ruins after the disastrous 1755 earthquake. For Vila Real he adopted the same grid pattern, paving and uniform facades as he used in Lisbon's Baixa quarter. All the materials (even the hewn stone and prefabricated window and door frames) were carted from the capital – the irony being that, a short while later, stone quarries were discovered in the vicinity of Vila Real. Make for the main Praça do Marquês de Pombal, a handsome square with black and white mosaic paving radiating from a central obelisk. Here you can sit under one of the sweet-smelling orange trees lining the square or order a drink in one of the open-air cafes.

Head two blocks east and cross the main Avenida da República into well-watered gardens. Watch ferries plying across the water, waders nosing in the mud and the whitewashed houses of Ayamonte on the Spanish side of the river. Go north up the Avenida, past some dignified residences on your left with Macau roofs (pitched and curved in Chinese fashion), and make for the tourist office on the esplanade near the ferry terminal. Check here for times of ferry crossings. Boats leave every half hour in summer, hourly in winter.

Once in Ayamonte, there is plenty of time to browse around the shops. There are no great bargains here, but plenty of Spanish souvenirs and places serving *paella*. If you stay for lunch, take a taxi up to the **Parador Costa de la Luz**, surveying a wide sweep of Spain and Portugal.

19. Beside the Guadiana

Castle at Castro Marim; riverside route to Alcoutim; scenic drive through the Serra do Caldeirão; sundowner at São Brás.

This tour takes you through some of the loveliest river and mountain scenery of the Algarve. Fill up the car before you set off — petrol stations are scarce where you will be going. To put the area into perspective, start the day at the hilltop castle of **Castro Marim**. The gate opens at 9am (closed holidays) but there is no need to be here before mid-morning (early risers can always breakfast in the border town of Vila Real de Santo António). Climb up to the battlements for good views of the River Guadiana, the natural frontier between Portugal and Spain. The international bridge spanning the Guadiana opened in 1992 and the IP1 motorway now goes as far as Albufeira. To the east you can see the Spanish border town of Ayamonte; to the south Vila Real; and just below you the flat saltpans of the region's **nature reserve**, where you might spot a stork or a black-winged stilt. For information on rarer species, ask at the nature reserve information office at the castle entrance.

The ancient fortress on a hillock to the southwest and what remains of the castle are clues that Castro Marim was once more

Saltpans around Vila Real

than a sleepy whitewashed village. The settlement dates back at least to the Phoenicians but the town played its key role in history as the headquarters in 1321 of the Knights of Christ – crucial contributors in the first phase of the Great Discoveries. You can pick up local background information in the **museum** within the castle walls. If shut, ask for the key at the nature reserve office.

Leave Castro Marim by noon and take the N122 marked to Beja and Mértola. The road climbs through remote rolling hills and over dried-up tributaries of the Guadiana. Another 6 km (4 miles) beyond Azinhal take the turning right marked Alcoutim and follow the road through cistus-covered hillsides where you are unlikely to see any life other than a herd of goats. Keep going for around 6 km (4 miles) and you reach the placid waters of the Gaudiana, with views across to the hills of Andalusia. Slow down to watch peaceful scenes of locals tilling the lush land by the river or tending vines.

At **Foz de Odeleite** the pastel-washed houses huddle on the hillside, patios brimming with oleander and geraniums. Follow the road along the river, past fields of corn, olive groves and patches of vines. Stop at **Guerreiros do Rio**, a primitive sleepy riverside village where chickens scratch among the cobbles and shelter from the heat in makeshift huts. The roads here are just potholed dirt tracks.

Slow down 3 km (2 miles) further on for fine views of the Moorish fortress and village of Sanlúcar de Guadiana on the Spanish side

The Guadiana river

of the river. **Alcoutim**, similarly crowned by castle ruins, soon comes into view on your side of the river. A couple of right turns bring you into the village square. Park and take the steps between the cafe and the bank up to the castle for views across the river. Return to the square and walk down to the landing stage where yachts are moored. Look across to Sanlúcar and you might spot a couple of storks nesting on top of the twin belfries of the church. The cafe/restaurant **O Soeiro** (next to the church and waterfront, closed weekends) is a good choice for lunch. Grab a riverview table, watch what's cooking on the brazier outside or see what the Portuguese are eating, then follow suit, washing everything down with Real Sassador wine. With time in hand find a fisherman with a boat to explore the waters upstream (ask at the tourist office near the landing stage) or visit the little **Museo do Rio**; but make

Castro Marim

sure you leave Alcoutim by 3.30pm. It is 84 km (52 miles) to São Brás de Alportel and you will be stopping en route.

Leaving Alcoutim, go up the hill and along the N122-1 till you come to the crossroads. Go straight over for Cachopo. Eucalyptus trees line the roadside and in spring the white flowers of rock roses and yellow splashes of broom dot the hillsides. The village of **Gilões** (marked off the main road 18 km (11 miles) beyond the crossroads) is the home of the last surviving basket weaver. Ask at the whitewashed Centro de Saude on your right as you go into the village and you may see him at work. One hat takes him up to two days to make. Further east and off the main road at **Martim Longo**, an industrious team of girls handmake sackcloth dolls. You will find them at the back of the blue and white *artesanato* shop as you fork right into the centre of the village. Dolls cost 1,200$ if you buy direct. A few doors on you will find more seamstresses, but this time at machines, making raw silk outfits, for good prices if you buy direct.

A detour south from Martim Longo towards Vaqueiros takes you deeper into the mountains until you come to Parque Mineiro Cova dos Mouros (tel: 289-999229, open daily 10.30am–6.30pm, entrance 2,000$00). In addition to some old mines, there is a wildlife park, pony treks and a traditional village on view. After Martim Longo, the road descends from the plateau, snaking and bumping its way through the pretty rolling landscape to Cachopo. Stop at one of the cafes here, then take the N124

Sanlúcar de Guadiana

to Barranco do Velho, a beautiful route with wooded valleys, stepped hillsides, pines and cistus shrubs. At Barranco do Velho take the left fork and follow the road down to São Brás de Alportel in the foothills of the Serra do Caldeirão. The cork trees here bear numbers denoting dates of bark stripping. Just 2 km (1¼ miles) before you reach São Brás, turn left at the sign for the **Pousada de São Brás** (Tel: 289-842305). This state-run hotel has beautiful views across the hills, down to the coast. If the place appeals, stay for dinner and try a Portuguese dish (the *caldeirada de borrego*, a lamb stew). The cafe-like **Luís dos Frangos** (nicknamed King of the Chickens) in São Brás on the Tavira road is far less formal, and a great place to meet the Portuguese. The speciality is barbecued chicken, with salad, chips and cheap wine, served at noisy communal tables.

Eating OUT

The Portuguese love food. Eating, whether at home or in a restaurant, is a highly sociable and frequently noisy occasion. A family outing to a favourite restaurant on a Sunday, or to celebrate a baptism, birthday or for almost any other reason, helps maintain the prominent position food has in local life.

In general, restaurant food is good, based on fresh local produce, and portions range from generous to (for the non-Portuguese) overwhelming; indeed, you may consider doing as the locals sometimes do and order a half portion – *meia dose* – or share a whole portion between two. Some of the best value-for-money dining will be found in the simplest restaurants away from the main tourist centres. Don't automatically be put off by outside appearances; if a restaurant is busy with locals, the food inside will usually be good. Service will almost invariably be welcoming and helpful.

Fish

Contrary to popular belief, there's a lot more to Algarve cuisine than a plate of fresh sardines and salad. It may not rank in the league of gourmet cuisine but there are plenty of good things about it, not the least the liberal use of marinades and spices (a legacy of the Portuguese Empire) and the sheer variety of fish.

Fish markets along the coast are laid

out with bass and bream, swordfish and scabbard fish, mackerel and mullet, crab claws and crayfish, starfish and spider crabs, cockles and clams – and more besides. Restaurants entice you with their tanks of live lobsters and piles of succulent prawns; and in summer sardines sizzles on barbecues all along the coast, served up with salad and crusty bread.

Fish is frequently marinaded in wine, olive oil or herbs, then simply grilled or barbecued. Alternatively they form the basis of wholesome fish soups and casseroles. The Algarve speciality is *amêijoas na cataplana*, a soup/casserole of clams, sausage, ham, garlic, herbs, spices and white wine, served in a *cataplana* – a special domed tin or copper vessel, rather like an old-fashioned pressure cooker. Look out too for *cataplana* dishes with lobster, *tamboril* (monkfish) or clams with pork. The minimum order is usually for two and is often ample for three or four. The same applies to *caldeirada*, which is like a French *bouillabaisse* and uses a variety of fish with onions, tomatoes, potatoes and paprika. *Arroz de marisco* (shellfish with rice and spices) is served in huge portions and is usually value for money.

Lobsters are whisked off by restaurateurs before they reach the market and inevitably fetch high prices. Fresh sea bream is excellent, as is swordfish (*espadarte*) served in steaks and grilled. Beware of 'fresh swordfish' served at any time other than in January and February, when it is caught. It will either be frozen swordfish or mako shark in disguise. Confusingly similar in name but entirely different to look at is *peixe espada*, the long, skinny 'scabbard fish' with pointed snout and silvery skin. This fish is sliced diagonally and then grilled.

Less appetising, at least to foreign tastes, are dishes made with *bacalhau* (dried cod), the most widely available fish dish in Portugal. The grey slabs hanging in shops and market stalls may not entice you, but the locals love this fish and have been eating it since the explorations in Newfoundland began in 1501. As every guide book will tell you, there are as many different ways of cooking dried cod as there are days in the year. When well prepared, *bacalhau* can be excellent and you will be completely unaware that it has been salt dried; on the other hand, if poorly prepared, it can, to a foreigner, be almost inedible. To avoid disappointment it is best sampled with the help of reliable local knowledge. Many of the dishes based on *bacalhau* are quite rich and heavy.

The big ports of Olhão and Portimão are excellent for fish restaurants. Also worth investigating are the **Rui Marisqueira** in Silves (tel: 282-442682, closed Tues) and the **O Lotus** in Lagoa (tel: 282-352098, closed Sat lunch). Both are excellent for fish, patronised by the Portuguese and not overpriced. Expect to pay around 2,500$ for an average three-course meal with wine.

Meat

As for meat, good grazing land is virtually non-existent and beef can be unpredictable in quality. Generally the best cut is 'lombo' but even so, beef and steaks are often disappointingly tough. Chicken may look scrawny but is full of flavour and always a safe bet. It is often marinaded, then barbecued (*frango no churrasco*). The ubiquitous chicken *piri-piri* uses a sauce made from chilli peppers, which can be mild and tangy or as strong as a Vindaloo. Like Indian curry spices, the hot sauce was once used in the African colonies to stop meat from spoiling or to hide its bad taste. However, don't let that put you off this tasty dish.

Monchique has numerous restaurants specialising in *piri-piri*. Try the **Restaurante Central** in the Caldas de Monchique or the **Paraiso da Montanha** on the Fóia road. Of the various self-styled 'kings of the chickens', the **Luís dos Frangos** on the Tavira road in São Brás de Alportel is one of the best. Unprepossessing and informal, the place does a roaring trade every night in barbecued meats. But the king of the kings of chicken has to be **O Teodosio** in Guia, a town sprawling along the N125 northwest of Albufeira, whose reputation is built entirely around *piri-piri*. Expect to pay around 1,500$ a head for a meal including half a bottle of Reguengos or Vidiguera wine. An alternative is to buy one of the very delicious spit-roasted chickens in the market or by the

roadside. One of these, together with fruit, bread and wine, makes a good picnic.

Pork is the main meat alternative to chicken. The Portuguese eat pork in all its different forms, from whole roast suckling pig to trotters with coriander. Try *carne de porco com amêijoas* (pork and clams), frequently cooked in a *cataplana*. Lamb may be bony but is good stewed. Kid is either roasted or casseroled with onions, tomatoes and potatoes – *cabrito estufado*. This is the speciality of the simple **Restaurant Adega Cova**, Vale d'Eguas in Almansil (tel: 289-395281, closed Tuesday and holidays).

Restaurants

Portuguese restaurants tend to be simple, set with paper tablecloths (useful for totting up the *escudos*) and baskets of coarse country bread, saucers of small black olives and perhaps a tin or two of sardine pâté and a little pot of cheese. If that does not suffice as a starter, try the *presunto* (delicious smoked ham, another speciality of Monchique, sometimes served with melon, *gaspacho*, the equivalent of the Spanish soup of the same name) or, on a cool day, *caldo verde* (a popular soup from the north

of Portugal). Nearer to home is the *sopa Alentejana* – full of garlic and with a poached egg floating in it.

A few years ago one would have rarely seen vegetables or salads being served in restaurants. Such produce abounds in the local markets, but traditionally vegetables and many salad ingredients would end up in the soup pot. Today you can generally get good salads (usually tempered with an oil and vinegar dressing) and at least one vegetable with a hot meal.

Along the coast the big resorts provide everything from fish and chips to five-star international cuisine. The stars may well denote an elegantly laid table and great service, but are not necessarily indicative of the quality of the food. Prices are markedly higher than those north of the N125, and menus are nearly always translated into English.

Some people maintain that the restaurant *par excellence* in the Algarve is **La Réserve**, at Santa Bárbara de Nexe (tel: 289-999234, closed Tuesday). The setting is refined and the food (for the most part French) is good, but it's very expensive. In recent years, the number of restaurants offering international cuisine has mushroomed, especially in larger towns. So, if you suddenly feel like a change of diet you'll find plenty of restaurants offering Chinese (especially dishes from Macau), Indian (dishes from Goa) and other national foods. Most will also offer Portuguese cuisine.

Eggs, Sugar and Almonds

The Portuguese sweet tooth is a legacy of the Moors, who introduced almond trees to Portugal and mixed the nuts with egg yolks to make sweetmeats. Several centuries later the enthusiasm for all things sweet was fuelled by the sugar plantations in Madeira. In the 17th/18th century convents were famed for their pastries, and the nuns handed down wonderful-sounding specialities such as as *toucinho do céu* (bacon from heaven) or *barriga de freira* (nun's belly). Today the Algarve's almonds and figs form the basis of many dozens of desserts and sweets. Marzipan is moulded into myriad shapes, from baby chicks to chessboards. To sample the sweets or fancy cakes and pastries stop at a *pastelaria*. Specialities unique to the Algarve are *Dom Rodrigo* and *Morgado*.

Tarte de amêndoa (almond tart), which is served at most Portuguese restaurants, is invariably good and there's the occasional orange tart. These are more inspiring than the selection of ice creams (usually itemised on large plastic menus) or the old stand-by, *pudim flan* – crème caramel. Few other desserts are likely to be available, unless you happen to be in an up-market international restaurant. However, fresh fruit is now widely served with a much wider choice than a few years ago. Oranges (with a little sugar) have a real tang to them and strawberries are usually excellent (try them doused in port wine – you'll never want them without again!).

Wine, Port and Liqueurs

The best thing about Algarve wine is its price. A litre costs as little as 300$. There are two reasons why you don't see a lot of it in restaurants: first, the lack of space between mountains and sea severely limits production; second, the wine's general lack of charm. Try it if you like with a picnic or plate of sardines, but watch out for the effects – 13 or 13.5 percent strength is quite normal. The biggest producer is **Lagoa,** which bottles mainly red, but also white, rosé and a golden aperitif wine called both **Alfonso III** and **Algar Seco.** You can visit the large wine cooperative in the town of Lagoa, east of Portimão, and watch the labels being glued on by hand (no tasting apart from groups).

Wines from the **Alentejo** (often served as the *vinho da casa*) are superb value. The red table wines from this region are currently some of the best produced in Portugal, the region having significantly upgraded quality in recent years – in contrast to some of the older established and well-known producing areas, which have tended to stand still in this respect. Alentejo labels you are most likely to come across are **Navegante** and **Terras d'el Rei**, and the full-bodied, dark **Real Vinicula** and **Borba** reds, not unlike Spanish wines.

Don't leave the Algarve without trying Portugal's more famous reds: the smooth, slightly sweet **Dão** (a well-established wine now making a comeback), its up-and-coming rival **Bairrada** (with a growing reputation for whites too) and the ruby-red **Colares**, which can be wonderful if aged. The **Douro valley** is producing some excellent quality lighter reds alongside the region's far more famous port wine.

One of the most characteristic Portuguese wines (far more so than the famous Mateus Rosé) is the light and *pétillant* **Vinho Verde** from the Minho region – a refreshing drink on any occasion. *Verde* refers to the age and not the colour (you can get white or red, although the latter is to be avoided). The wines are drunk very young, usually no later than the spring or summer after the harvest.

White wines tend not to keep well and anything more than three years old needs to be chosen with care. Excellent young whites are being produced in the **Ribatejo** and **Setubal Peninsula**. Whilst Mateus Rosé is synonomous with Portugal outside the country, it is never drunk by the locals! If you order some with your dinner, you are confirming your status as a visitor.

End your meal with a Portuguese brandy, liqueur or port. The Algarve specialities are the potent **Medronho**, distilled from the berries of the *Arbutus unedo* tree, which you see growing in profusion around Monchique, **Algarviana**, made from almonds, and **Branydmel**, a honey-based liqueur. Port is seldom drunk by the locals and is not as cheap as you might imagine. If you are curious, try some of the different types and vintages at the **Caves do Vinho do Porto** in Rua da Liberdade 23, Albufeira, or at the Artisans' Village on the N125 between Alcantarilha and Porches (free wine tasting).

White port (*porto branco*), frequently dismissed by wine buffs as being inferior to its more celebrated relative, makes an excellent aperitif when served chilled. Go for the drier, paler varieties. The exotic dessert wine **Madeira** (produced on the island of the same name) is the only wine to be heated in a special oven or *estufa* before being consumed. There are four basic types of Madeira: light, dry, rich and sweet.

Cafes, Snacks and Picnics

In Portuguese cafes look for the day's dishes scribbled up on blackboards. These may be a plate of sardines, a mixed salad, a nourishing stew and a simple omelette. After a lot of dew or rain you may see a notice on bars and cafes for snails *(caracois)*, which the locals eat with beer. Coffee is invariably good. Ask for *uma bica* (espresso), *um garoto* (small with milk) or *um galão* (large with milk).

For a snack or main meal you can also try a *cervejaria* (somewhere between a cafe and a restaurant) or a *marisqueira* (specialises in seafood). Whether self-catering or preparing a picnic, markets are invariably the best source. They are open from 8am–12.30/1pm. Choose cold meats from the hanging rows of *chouriços* (sausages), *presunto* (smoked ham) and fresh fruits. Typical cheeses are *queijo da Serra* (made from ewes' milk and matured in wood cellars) or *cabreiro* (goats' cheese).

Bread is available at all the larger markets; alternatively make your way to a local bakery for big crusty rolls, rough country loaves or bread that is flavoured with pork.

Food Vocabulary

Entradas (starters) and *sopa* (soup)

presunto = smoked ham
gambás = langoustines
camarão = prawn
santola recheada = dressed crab
pasteis de bacalhau = dried cod fishcakes
amêijoas = clams
rissóis de camarão = small shrimp pies
caldo verde = cabbage and potato soup
    with sliced sausage
sopa de coentros = coriander, bread and
    poached egg soup
creme de marisco = seafood soup
canja = chicken broth

Peixe (fish)

caldeirada de peixe = fish stew
salmonete = red mullet
sardinhas grelhadas com pimentos =
    grilled sardines and peppers
bacalhau á Brás = fried dried codfish
    served with fried potatoes and scram-
    bled eggs
lagosta = lobster
lampreia = lamprey
lulas recheadas = stuffed squid
atum grelhado = grilled tuna fish
arroz de polvo = octopus with rice
ensopado de enguias = eels served with
    fried bread
robalo = sea bass
rodovalho = hallibut
linguado = sole
salmão = salmon
truta = trout
savel = shad

Carne (meat)

carne assada = roast beef
arroz de pato = duck with rice
cozido à portuguesa = variety of boiled
    meats and vegetables
cabrito assado = roast kid
frango na pucara = chicken casserole
arroz à moda de Valência = kind of paella
frango de carril = roast chicken served
    with a hot sauce
churrasco = pork cooked on a spit
coelho à caçadora = rabbit stew
tripas à moda do Porto = tripe served with
    dried beans
feijoada = dried beans with rice and
    various smoked meats.
leitão assado = roast sucking pig
prego = steak sandwich
porco = pork
vitela = veal
peru = turkey

Salada (salad)

alface = lettuce
tomate = tomatoe
pepino = cucumber
cebola = onion
cenoura = carrot

Doces (sweets)

queijo = cheese
marmelada = quince marmalade
papos de anjo = small butter cakes served
    with syrup
arroz doce = sweet rice
leite creme = type of custard
pudim flan = cream caramel
fruta = fruit
maça = apple
morangos = strawberries
pera = pear
laranja = orange
uvas = grapes

Basic foods

vinagre = vinegar
alho = garlic
azeite = olive oil
azeitona = olive
manteiga = butter
pão = bread
pão integral = wholemeal bread
pimenta = pepper
sal = salt
açucar = sugar

Nightlife

Twenty-five years ago nightlife in the Algarve amounted to no more than a glass of wine or Medronho in a little *adega* or, at its liveliest, an evening of music, song and dance at a local *festa*. However, with the advent of tourism came the invasion of discos and nightclubs. With local wine and beer at giveaway prices, late night bars began to flourish. Today, nightlife consists of dozens of discos, three casinos, various cabarets and occasional folklore and *fado* nights. Prices are no longer cheap. Unless you are a single woman (who may be admitted free) expect to pay anything from 1,000$ to 6,000$ for entrance to a night-club (first drink included). In any disco be prepared to wait until 1am for things to hot up.

Discos

The hottest spot is Albufeira, which throbs to the beat of discos until the early hours of the morning. The majority of these are undistinguished, with earsplitting music, loud tourists or hot-blooded Portuguese in the inevitable pursuit of foreign female talent. Discos go in and out of fashion with remarkable rapidity. Among the most popular at present are **Kiss**, at Montechoro near Albufeira, **Kadoc**, on the outskirts of Vilamoura (a vast disco with an open air terrace) and **Locomia** at Santa Eulalia, east of Albufeira, which lures young, well-heeled Portuguese. Entrance here is free, but bar prices are steep. The key feature is a giant champagne bottle, suspended from the ceiling, which intermittently spews forth a great stream of foam, filling the dance floor and providing a good excuse for shedding a garment.

Further east, at Quinta do Lago, you can rub shoulders with the jet set at the **Pátio** night club – providing you are willing to pay a minimum of 5,000$. There is no entrance charge; the bill is surreptitiously settled as you leave. Other places to try for good music and ambience are **Horta 2** (between Portimão and Odiáxere), **Phoenix** in Lagos, **Trigonometria** in Quinta do Lago, **Privé** in Praia da Luz and **UBI** in Tavira.

Casinos

Lay your bets at **Vilamoura**, **Monte Gordo** or **Alvor**. Passports or ID cards are essential and men should wear jackets. Gaming rooms open in the early evening for roulette, blackjack, French bank and slot machines. There are also three-course meals and cabaret, starting at around 5,000$. Gaming rooms close at 3 or 4am.

Bars

The tourist boom along the coast has brought a steady proliferation of bars catering for cosmopolitan tastes. English

and Irish expatriates have set up pubs serving British and Irish beer, along with exotic cocktails. Many bars lure customers with a Happy Hour, when two drinks are served for the price of one.

Try **The Lionheart** (Rua do Castelo dos Governadores, 12, Lagos) where they offer foreign brand beers, music, TV sport and bar snacks to the early hours. If you overdo it take heart – Lagos Hospital is right opposite. In Portimão try the **Bar e Bar** on the beach at Praia da Rocha; this is young and relaxed, and lots of fun.

If snooker's your scene, try **O Montinho** at Montechoro (just west of Albufeira). For Brazilian music and drinks try **Os Arcos** in Rua do Prior, Faro.

Fado

Lamentations of lost loves, lovers crossed and the forces of destiny are all characteristic themes of the Portuguese *fado*. Sung by professionals, these chants are plangent, haunting and intensely moving. To the unattuned ear they can sound monotonous, hence the jollification of traditional *fado* for the benefit of tourists in the Algarve. Authentic *fado* has its roots in the university town of Coimbra and in Lisbon (country and coast folk sang songs of the weather, crops and sea; city folk of love), and it is in the cafes and restaurants of the *Bairro Alto* quarter of the capital that you are more likely to hear the real thing.

If you are keen to see a performance in the Algarve, consult local English-language magazines and newspapers such as the *Algarve Gazette* and the *Algarve News* for venues. The **Sol e Mar Hotel** in the centre of Albufeira, the **O Muralho** at the top of the Rua Infante de Sagres in Lagos and the **Hotel Eva** in Faro are three of the main ones, all tourist-orientated. Alternatively, you may catch a gifted *fado* singer giving an impromptu performance in a village restaurant.

Folk Dancing

The regional folk dances are colourful affairs performed with vigour and enthusiasm, but rarely on a professional level. The groups are formed in local villages and most of the dancers work in the daytime as maids, labourers or builders. Music is usually provided by a vocalist accompanied by an accordion, a *cavaquinhos* (small guitar-like instruments), triangle and drum.

Occasionally you may hear a *desafio* (challenge) where two singers ad-lib verses in turn, the one trying to outdo the other. Obviously to really appreciate this you need to know the language and, since often the challenges will include references to local people or events, some help may be needed to explain what's causing the hilarity amongst the listeners; nevertheless the sheer enjoyment and participation of the local audience is entertainment enough in itself.

The traditional folk dance of the region is the *corridinho*, a lively country dance despite the fact that the dancers wear black costumes. Local publications will give you details of folk dancing venues (the **Fonte Pequena Folklore Centre** in Alte – *see Itinerary 10* – is one of the main places). Very often local *festas* will include at least one night of dancing (called a *baille* or ball). These can be great fun and will include local traditional music (live or recorded). Young and old alike attend and the dancing can be quaintly formal. Regular *bailles* are held in the summer months on Saturday nights by Poço Barreto railway station and in the square at Ferragudo village. Usually you can buy some food from the temporary stalls, barbecued chicken being a particularly tasty and ever-popular option. Locating *festas* otherwise is a case of asking at the tourist office – or simply listening out for the noise.

Shopping

Whatever you want to shop for, whether it's fashion clothing, handicrafts or foodstuffs, there's a good chance that you'll find what you're looking for somewhere in the Algarve. The boom in tourism and presence of a significant international resident population has resulted in an excellent range of shopping facilities, ranging from the simplest colourful local market through to hypermarkets and specialist stores trading under internationally known names and offering products sold in all the major cities of the world.

Shops are usually open Monday to Friday 9am–1pm and 3–7pm and Saturday 9am–1pm. In the summer months these times can be significantly extended. Hypermarkets and out-of-town shopping centres will usually be open until 10pm and also on Sundays and public holidays.

If you leave shopping to the very last minute, remember that Faro Airport has good facilities.

The best buys are handicrafts: wickerwork, ceramics, embroidery, rugs, copper, brass, wrought iron, woodwork and leather. Along the coast, where souvenir shops and stalls do a roaring trade in cheap baskets from China, you are unlikely to catch a glimpse of that dying breed, the Algarve artisan. Weavers transforming sisal fibres into baskets and hampers, craftsmen beating copper and brass, and ladies making lace at their doorways are fast disappearing. Inland, however, you will still occasionally find surviving artisans producing the genuine articles *(see Itineraries 11 and 19)*. The *artesanato* stalls dotted all along the N125 are fun to browse.

Check in local English-language magazines for the dates of weekly markets and fairs. These are large colourful affairs, where you can pick up reasonably priced pottery, basketry, linen and lace. The big gipsy markets sell everything from fresh mountain cheeses to old liquor stills and pots of snake oil. For the locals a visit to the weekly market is not only an occasion to buy and sell, it is also the social highlight of the week – a whole day of looking, bartering, gossiping, eating and drinking, at the end of which they will plod wearily home laden with the day's acquisitions.

Markets tend to have distinct sectors for food, clothing, tools and implements, livestock and so on. They can give great insight into the local economy and way of life, so an hour or two spent wandering around one is always productive, even if you don't buy anything. If you do want to make a purchase, ask the price first

Leather working

and be prepared to haggle or walk away. The first price you are given will drop significantly. Don't feel too badly about this: the locals do it and, in any case, you will still almost inevitably be paying more than a local would!

Antiques

For sheer amusement try the **Casa do Papagaio** at Rua 25 de Abril in Lagos, stacked with priceless Portuguese antiques and dusty religious artefacts, which look as though they should be in a museum. They also have a second shop in Lagos, in Rua Lanzarote de Freitas, 24. In Portimão try **A Tralha** in Largo do Dique, 15 or Rua João de Deus, 1, for antiques and Madeira embroideries. For something entirely different, the roadside *artesanato* on the N125 (soon after the Loulé turn-off if you are travelling east–west) sell an interesting collection of old ploughs, cart wheels, liquor stills and a host of other rural bygones.

Basketry

Baskets range from the cheap imported variety to those that have taken a local two days to make. To see Algarve weavers at work turn off the N125 at Boliqueime to the road for Loulé and (dependent on time of year and day) you may well see them busily working by the roadside. Buy direct. (See also Itinerary 19, which takes you through mountain villages where a few basket-makers and other craftsmen survive.) The **Artenesato Regional Bazaar** (Tavira) has a good selection of typical Portuguese ratten baskets. In the eastern end of the Algarve, there are still several basket-makers at work in and around the villages of Alcoutim and Odeleite.

Ceramics

Arguably the best buy (though also the most cumbersome to carry home) are ceramic pieces. The choice is endless, from china in the shape of roosters (a kind of national symbol), mini-chimneys, snails and vine leaves to Greek and Roman-style *amphorae*. Pictorial *azulejos*, the glazed Portuguese tiles, make attractive gifts, though the old ones do tend to be somewhat overpriced.

The potteries at Porches, sprawled along the N125, are the best source for variety. Try **Casa Algarve** or **Porches Pottery** (open Monday–Friday all day, Saturday 10am–1pm, 4–6pm, 7pm in summer), which competes with its large range of floral-patterned hand-painted *majolica (see box on page 78)* and has the added advantage of an inviting bar *in situ*. Traditions here have been handed down over the centuries – at least until the 1960s, when metal and plastic took over and becoming a potter became *infra dig*. In 1968 an Irishman, Patrick Swift, revived a dying industry by decorating plain pottery and selling it to the tourists beginning to invade the Algarve. The *majolica* is all hand-painted (you can see the girls at work) and patterns are all variations on traditional designs.

The Porches Pottery owners Kate Swift and Roger Metcalfe have a studio (**Estudio Destra**) in the centre of Silves (tel: 282-442983). They produce hand-painted *majolica*, featuring traditional patterns combined with contemporary themes.

In the Algarve the choice of ceramics is complex. Cheapest is the local glazed terracotta pottery bordered with a white floral line and widely used by the Portuguese. But keep a look-out too for pottery from other regions of Portugal. Coimbra's hand-painted pottery depicting animals and birds in floral settings is notable. Then there is the distinctive and decorative Alentejo pottery, often illustrated with flowers, fish or simple scenes from daily life.

MAJOLICA

The word *majolica* comes from a 19th-century trade-name (also spelt *maiolica*) for earthenware with coloured decorations on an opaque white glaze. The technique had its origins in Majorca and Valencia, and has an obvious Moorish flavour in many of the patterns.

Tin and lead oxides (both are found in Iberia) are the basic ingredients of the glaze, produced when they melt together. The formed clay body or biscuit is dipped into the oxide mix and a thin film of glaze deposited on the surface. The patterns, with their traditional vivid colours, are then painted on to the white glaze surface. Blues and yellows are particularly widely used, these pigments also being based on metal oxides available within Iberia.

The painted piece will receive a final transparent over-glaze, and will be fired in the kiln to set the finished glazes.

Those with designer taste should consider picking up Leiria pottery with its bright, bold decoration (usually fish and flowers). For an unusual selection of antique-styled Portuguese earthenware (in addition to a range of modern designs), you should pay a visit to the **Infante D Henrique House** at No 30, Rua Cândido dos Reis, Albufeira.

Copper and Brass

If you stroll around the Rua 9 de Abril or Rua da Barbacã in Loulé, you are still likely to hear the beating of brass and copper. Craftsmen here work in tiny workshops and the nearby shops are full of their copper and brass pots and pans. Look out for old liquor stills – these make a really unusual purchase – and *cataplanas* (if you want to try your hand at cooking Algarve specialities at home) sold at *artesanato* stalls on the EN125 roadside, for example, between Olhão and Tavira.

Crystal

The old Portuguese art of glass-making still survives. Today the big name in the business is Atlantis, who make a Portuguese full-lead crystal. **O Aquário** on the corner of Rua Vasco da Gama and Praça de República, in Portimão, stocks top quality crystal and sells in addition Vista Alegre, which is the finest porcelain in Portugal.

Embroidery, Lace and Weaving

'Where there are nets, there is lace' goes the local saying. You certainly see plenty of it along the coast but not a great deal is actually hand-made these days. Good buys in shops and stalls are colourful heavy bedspreads, rugs and curtains from the Alentejo. Look out too for handwoven carpets from Arraiolos, north of Evora. The best venue for these is **Arraiolos**, Rua Dr Teófilo Braga, next to the Town Hall in Portimão, who make to order and ship abroad. Look too in markets for woven mats or rugs selling for as little as 500$.

To see locals weaving, try the first tower on your left as you go into the castle at Silves where women work at looms making tablecloths, bedspreads, etc. Orders can be taken and shipped directly to your home address. Villagers still crochet in their spare time but rarely for the benefit of tourists. Their bedspreads with fine patterns are often tucked away in trunks and cupboards. However, it is

Souvenir hunting

Cheese stall in Loulé

possible to come across lace-makers and buy some fine examples of the hand-made articles in and around the village of Azinhal, near the Spanish border at the eastern end of the Algarve. For good-quality bedcovers, try looking in the nearby village of Tacões.

The only practical way of buying direct is to enquire in the villages who embroiders or crochets: the Portuguese for this is *Onde posso encontrar uma senhora que saiba fazer colchas e toalhas de mesa em crochet?*

Food and Wine

Tio José in Praça da República, Portimão, boasts the 'largest selection of Portuguese port, wines and brandies'. The excellent Bairrada wines are good travellers. Good years are 1975, '77, '82, '83, '85, '91, '94, '95 and '96. At **The Artisans Village** (on the N125 between Porches and Alcantarilha) you can have free wine tasting and then buy from the comprehensive selection available, as well as look around (and buy) handicrafts from the region. Avoid the duty-free drink shops — these are not really worth bothering with unless you want to buy foreign spirits.

Markets are a good source for cheeses, hams, sausages and fresh food generally. Sweets made of almonds, marzipan and figs are sold everywhere.

Golf Shops

If you want to buy (or in some cases just rent) golfing equipment you are spoilt for choice, as there are a number of large specialist stores to chose from. These include **Florida Golf** (on the N125 at Vale d'Eguas outside Almancil), **Golfers Paradise** (in the centre of Almancil) and **Planet Golf** (in the Avenida 5 de Outubro in Almancil).

Jewellery

One of the best buys is marcasite, a legacy of the Moors. Small rings start for as little as 1,000$. Look also for filigree work, an old Portuguese craft. Pliable silver and gold wire is still fashioned into shapes such as birds and flowers. For imaginative designs in jewellery try the following shops: **Mogodor**, Rua Gil Eanes, Lagos; **Terracotta**, Praça Luís de Camões, Lagos; and **Stárte**, Rua Guilherme Gomes Fernandes, No 26, Tavira (behind the cinema).

Leather

There are some good buys to be found if you are prepared to shop around a bit and you need to know what to look out for. Cheap bags in markets start at about 2,000$, but expect to pay at least 20,000$ for a top designer creation in a boutique. For shoes try the shops in Loulé, **Charles Jourdan at St James** in Portimão (Rua Santa Isabel) or Albufeira (Edifício Tural, Av de 25 Abril), for classical Parisian designs at low Portuguese prices. Other worthwhile places to investigate are **Gaby's**, at Rua Direita 5 and Praça Vicronde Bívar 15 in Portimão; **Via Gama**, Av Dr Sá Carneiro, Albufeira; and **Oberon** and **António Manuel Boutique** (soft leather jackets) in the Rua de Santo António in Faro.

Woollens

The best sources for chunky woollen cardigans and jumpers, patterned or plain, are (somewhat surprisingly) the stalls outside Sagres fortress and Cape St Vincent. The fisherman's jumpers and woolly socks are good quality excellent buys and make welcome presents; so do hand-dyed cotton jumpers (for recommended shopping in Portimão *see Itinerary 4, page 32*).

Sport

Sports enthusiasts are spoilt for choice in the Algarve. The region has all the ingredients for an active holiday: all-year sunshine, fine beaches for water sports, a choice of resorts with their own sports centres and a hinterland ribboned with some of the finest golf courses in Europe. Although the sea water is rather choppy for novices to water sports, it is often possible to practise on the calm waters of nearby lagoons. Increasingly, less obvious activities are being catered for, with walking itineraries, horse riding, diving and four-wheel drive 'safaris' all becoming widely available.

Golf

Not surprisingly the Algarve promotes itself as a golfer's paradise. There are 17 courses, eight of them championship standard, and there are more in the pipeline. But spiralling green fees and the incessant demand for preferential tee times, especially from May to October, are already putting some players off the game. At the exclusive new **San Lorenzo**, currently rated number two in continental Europe by *Golf World* magazine, the only hope of membership is to buy a plot, pay out the huge 6,000,000$ (£24,000) membership fee plus an extra 550,000$ (£2,200) every year. Green fees at the top venues are around 15,000$, and hence the courses are becoming more and more the exclusive domain of the international jet set.

If you are serious about playing, plan your trip with care. The only way to guarantee preferential tee times and secure green fee discounts is either to stay in a hotel affiliated with the course or to rent a villa on the fringes of the fairways. In summer, arrange your games for early morning or late afternoon to avoid the midday heat.

For up-to-date information, look for the VIP Algarve map, golfer's edition.

Main courses

QUINTA DO LAGO (tel: 289-390700). A 2,000 acre complex around the Quinta do Lago and Ria Formosa courses offering a total of 36 holes, a true test for golfers of all levels. Incorporates the most famous and probably the most exclusive course in the Algarve. The 1,500 sprinklers keep the greens in immaculate condition and the tees have been compared to bowling greens. Very scenic terrain with pine woods, lakes and wildlife. Trees and water (from fresh and saltwater pools) are the main hazards.

PENINA (tel: 282-415415). Has an 18-hole championship course and two nine-hole courses. The longest established course in the Algarve, designed by Henry Cotton. Beautifully landscaped course, lush greens with woods and strategically placed lakes and streams. Notorious short par-three 13th where, in 1986 dredgers in the lake uncovered around 20,000 lost balls. Five-star facilities include the Hotel Penina, tennis and pool.

SAN LORENZO (tel: 289-396534). An 18-hole championship course. Very exclusive, owned by Forte Hotels. Scenically similar to Quinta do Lago. To secure a game you have to stay either at the nearby Dona Filipa Hotel, the Penina Hotel, or own or rent one of the villas on the 2,000-acre estate at Quinta do Lago.

PINE CLIFFS (tel: 289-500100). This establishment opened in 1990. Luxury golf and country club with a nine-hole golf course, five-star Sheraton Hotel, large pool, villas and apartments, overlooking ravines and beach.

VALE DO LOBO (tel: 289-393939). Eighteen and nine-hole courses. Another course designed by Henry Cotton. The seventh hole on the Yellow Course, stretching 192m (210yds) over two ravines, is the most photographed in Europe. Some spectacular sea views from the Yellow and Orange courses.

VILAMOURA I – OLD COURSE (tel: 289-322650). Eighteen holes. Located among pine forests, with sea views. Venue of various championships.

VILAMOURA II – PINHAL (tel: 289-321562). An 18-hole course. Opened in 1976 but redesigned and enlarged since. Spectacular sea views from the first nine holes; back nine through umbrella pines.

VILAMOURA III – LAGUNA (tel: 289-310180). Three nine-hole courses.

PALMARES (tel: 282-762961). An 18-hole course near Lagos, with undulating terrain and spectacular views of the sea and hills. This fabulous venue is famous for the Almond Blossom Tournament.

PARQUE DE FLORESTA (tel: 282-690054). Another 18-hole course set in hills above Salema about 16 km/10 miles west of Lagos, the course offers a real challenge. A residential complex and hotel are also planned in the near future.

VILA SOL (tel: 289-300505). Eighteen-hole course, which hosted the Portuguese Open in 1992 and 1993.

PINHEIROS ALTOS (tel: 289-359910). Two sets of nine holes at Quinta do Lago.

SALGADO (tel: 289-583030). This is an

18-hole course reminiscent of a Scottish links course.

VAL DE MILHO (tel: 282-358502). Two nine-hole courses, which are cheaper than many others in the area.

GRAMACHO (tel: 282-340900). A double nine fairway course with two sets of tees and greens to each fairway, giving a total of 18 holes.

PINTA (tel: 282-340900). A beautifully planned course blending into undulating olive grove countryside.

ALTO GOLF (tel: 282-416913). Fine views of sea and hills. The last course to be designed by Sir Henry Cotton.

In addition to the above, just over the border in Spain (and nearer to Faro than Portimão) you have the choice of the Isla Canela and Islantilla courses.

Driving Ranges

BALAIA VILLAGE, near Albufeira. This impressive 50-bay driving range is open six days a week.

CLUB BARRINGTON, Vale do Lobo. This is a 29-bay, two-tiered driving range, open all week.

Riding

Ride across dunes and lagoons or trek in the hillsides. There are excellent schools, some English run. The superior stables at **Quinta do Lago** (Pinetrees tel: 289-396902) are run just like an English

riding school. There are pony rides, treks, hacks, beach rides and trips into the Ludo valley. **Paraiso dos Cavalos**, Almancil (tel: 289-394189) is one of the longest established riding centres in the whole of the Algarve.

Other ranches include the **Centro Hípico at Vilamoura** (tel: 289-322675); **Quinta Paraíso Alto** at Fronteira, 7 km (4 miles) north of Lagos (tel: 282-687263); and **Casa Galaraz – Centro Hípico** near Praia Carvoeira (tel: 282-358055). These schools usually cater for beginners and experienced riders but phone to check.

Water Sports

Windsurfing schools with instruction and board hire are located all along the coast. Real surfing is best along the west coast. Water-skiing is usually only available in the larger resorts and only in high season – telephone the local tourist information centre for details.

The main marina is at Vilamoura, where you can rent yachts and motor boats (tel: 289-312023), but there are plenty of other places for renting boats including Lagos (at the **Sailing Club**), Vila Real, Tavira and Faro. A good spot for those wanting to try their hand at windsurfing, water-skiing or sailing is the calm expanse of water on the Barragem do Arade near Silves. Equipment may be hired for the whole range of water sports at the **Sea Sports Centre** (tel: 282-789538) in Praia da Luz. Diving and sailing instruction,

fishing and boat trips are also available from this establishment.

Diving

Explore the underwater world of reefs and marine life just a stone's throw away from the shore. **Blue Ocean Divers** near Lagos (tel: 282-782718) put on professionally guided excursions. The diving centre **Estrela do Rio** at Areias de São João (tel: 289-588486) has facilities for beginners and experienced alike. At the **Sea Sports Centre** in Praia da Luz (tel: 282-789538) the German deep-sea diver Detlef Seager runs a diving centre and supplies equipment.

Paragliding and Microlighting

Lagos Aerodrome (tel: 282-762906) offers microlighting trips: 9,500$ (10 minutes), 16,500$ (20 minutes). Lessons are available at the aerodrome for both microlighting and paragliding. Another good spot for paragliding is the **Clube da Quinta,** Quinta do Lago, which features excellent views of the Ria Formosa nature reserve. For hot-air ballooning trips, contact Vistarama Flyer (tel: 289-316576) at Vilamoura. Trips start at around 3,000$.

Tennis

There are courts all along the coast. The main centre is the **Roger Taylor Tennis Club** at Vale do Lobo (tel: 289-589423), with 12 courts, restaurant and pool, plus instruction. Others include the **Hotel Montechoro** at Albufeira (tel: 289-589423) and the **Luz Bay Club**, Praia da Luz (tel: 282-789640). **Ténis da Quinta da Balaia**, just outside Albufeira (tel: 289-586575) has floodlit courts; the **Vilamouraténis Centre** (tel: 289-302369) occupies a central position and has 12 courts; the **Centro Ténis de Faro**, 2 km/1 mile from the airport (tel: 289-817877), has six floodlit courts .

Fishing

For big game fishing see Itinerary 5. Alternatively, try fishing from beaches, rocks, jetties or in the inland reservoirs. Equipment can be hired in most of the resorts. Fishermen occasionally take tourists out in their boats, either for serious fishing or a tour of the coastline and grottoes. Look out for notices on the beaches.

Water Parks

The huge water chutes resembling giant coloured snakes are the most eye-catching features along the N125. Prices at the water parks range from 1,600–2,800$ (adult) and 1,150–1,600$ (child) They may cover a full day or a half day.

THE BIG ONE, Alcantarilha, on the N125. Large park with slides and rides: corkscrew, raging rapids, flying carpets, wave pool, crazy leap (open May–September).

ATLANTICO, Quatro Estradas (between Quarteira and Loulé). Acapulco high-diving team in high season (open daily 10am–7pm).

WILD WATERS, Montechoro Park, Albufeira. Almost a mile of slides and rides; giant flumes and Australian tube slides; includes the Algarve's largest pool. Local transport is provided free of charge.

SLIDE & SPLASH, Lagoa (Estombar Road). This park offers four main slides plus double corkscrew, whirlpool, a waterfall and river ride (open May–September).

ZOO MARINE, on the N125 between Guia and Alcantarilha. Seals, dolphins and performing parrots as well as swimming pools. A big wheel and bouncy castles (open daily 10am–8pm).

Safaris

Jeep safaris into the inland areas of the Algarve are becoming increasingly popu-

lar and are a way to experience a totally different world from the coastal strip.

Operators include **Pangarb Tours** in Albufeira (tel: 289-515373) and **Rio Sail** (tel: 281-510200) in Monte Gordo. The latter also offers river cruises up the Guadiana River.

Walking

Increasingly, itineraries are being way-marked and books/leaflets published with walks for all levels of fitness. A long-distance footpath is being established along the whole length of the Algarve. More specialised interests are also starting to be catered for, for example, geological walks (tel: 289-890920).

Bullfighting

In 1799 the Portuguese Count of Arcos, one of the more foolhardy matadors of his day, was fatally injured in the ring. As a result the King of Portugal, deeming bullfighting to be an all too dangerous sport, declared that in future the bull's horns would be padded and the animal would always leave the ring alive. Since then Portuguese bullfights have been less violent affairs, with all the emphasis on the skill and elegance involved in taunting and subduing rather than slaying the bull. If this sounds preferable to the Spanish *corrida*, bear in mind that the bulls are often injured and usually slaughtered shortly after the fight.

The season lasts from May until October. Fights take place on Saturday at 5.30pm. Eye-catching posters on walls throughout the Algarve will announce any imminent fights, or you can find the dates in local magazines. Tickets may be bought at hotels or at the ring, and prices vary according to the position of the seats.

Bullfighting enthusiasts who have seen a fight in the Ribatejo, breeding ground of the best bulls, claim that Algarve fights are tame affairs aimed entirely at the tourists. This may be true but tourists who go claim to enjoy the spectacle for its sheer entertainment and (comparative) lack of gore, regardless of the quality of the bulls or fighters. The fact that the bull remains continuously active throughout the length of the fight (as opposed to the Spanish *corrida*, where the *picadores* can severely weaken the animal) makes it an eventful spectacle right through to the very end.

The fight begins with the *toureiro* (matador), decked out in flamboyant 18th-century costume, brandishing his red cape to bait the bull. Next to appear are the *cavaleiros* (horsemen on stallions), who stab the bull's shoulders with *farpas* (darts). The final act involves eight acrobatic *forcados* who run in to challenge the animal. The leader *(londroal)* goads the bull and hurls himself between its horns, while the rest of the team wrestle with the beast and bring it down to the ground. This is known as the *pegas*.

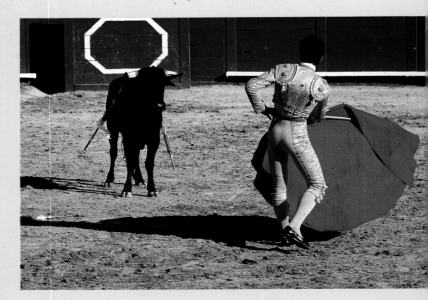

Calendar of Special Events

The Portuguese have a passion for public holidays, fairs and festivals, and the southerners are no exception. Dozens of towns and villages in the Algarve celebrate the local patron saint's day with parades, fireworks and plenty of merriment in the form of song and dance. Some are strictly religious, while others have become events aimed primarily at the tourists. Either way they are colourful, earthy events, well worth sampling if they happen to coincide with your visit.

To witness the more ethnic of the 'feast' days, seek out celebrations in the smaller villages where locals will insist you join in the merriment. Local tourist offices will provide you with regularly updated leaflets on events throughout the region.

January

'Charolas': Between New Year and Twelfth Night groups of singers and musicians holding up banners with ribbons and flowers roam through the streets of towns and villages singing traditional seasonal songs. The New Year's Day speciality, endorsing the Portuguese passion for sweet and sticky cakes, is a sugary bun, which is not unlike a doughnut.

Late February/Early March

Carnival is the year's big event. Celebrations begin four Saturdays before Shrove Tuesday with dancing in carnival costume, and culminate in three days of street merriment. It's a time when everyone lets off steam, pranksters throw rotten eggs and flour and neighbours say what they really think about each other. Largest and liveliest is the carnival at **Loulé** with its procession of colourful floats, marching bands and dancing groups. Deeply rooted in paganism, carnival tradi-

tionally celebrates the end of winter, and in some smaller villages you can still witness the mock 'burial' of winter. A 'corpse', either in the form of a real person or an effigy of death, is carried through the village streets, while black-clad villagers 'in mourning' follow behind. The 'corpse' is taken to the churchyard and ceremoniously buried or burned. Once the event is complete, winter is finally over, joy resumes and wild celebrations can begin.

March/April

Easter is celebrated with religious processions, typically led by a priest swinging a censer of burning herbs, with followers strewing symbolic flowers in the streets. Annual processions are held in **Faro, Alcantarilha, Algoz** and **Lagoa. São Brás de Alportel** has a colourful festival on Easter Sunday when the streets are strewn with flowers. The second Sunday after Easter the *Romaria e Festa da Mae Soberana* at **Loulé** is a strange and unique folk pilgrimage, intermingling pagan and Christian elements.

Anniversary of the 1974 Revolution: This event, on 25 April, commemorates the bloodless Carnation Revolution which overthrew the government *(see History section, page 19).*

May

May Day is celebrated by folk festivals in **Albufeira, Guia, Paderne, Alcoutim, Odeleite, Estômbar** and **Alte**. Join in the festivities, see folk dance competitions and buy from stalls selling local handicrafts and symbolic bunches of flowers. **Alte** is the main venue.

The Festa da Pinha (Pine Festival), from 1–3 May in **Estói,** dates back to the times when farmers travelled to the Alentejo by mule to trade. If they returned safely with the traded goods,

unscathed by bandits, the occasion was celebrated by feasting and drinking in the forests. Wine and beer still flow, along with barbecued chicken, dancers, accordianists and guitarists.

The Festa da Espiga in **Salir** is an old farming folk festival, held in the second week of May and celebrating fertility. Floats are traditionally decorated in green (symbolising crops) and red (symbolising poppies). The procession is followed by fireworks and folk dancing. Don't be surprised if you are handed a spray of plants – each one has a special significance.

May/June

The Algarve Music Festival, which is always held between May and June, now attracts international as well as Portuguese participants. The programme is suitably varied. Concerts and recitals are held in several venues: at the cathedral in **Silves**, the parish church in **Albufeira** and in other ecclesiastical venues offering good acoustics. The music festival also includes ballet performances.

June

Santos Populares (Saints Day) is traditionally a time when the locals 'come out' and make merry with dancing, music, food and drink. Streets throughout the Algarve are decorated with banners. In some villages rosemary is burnt and children jump over open fires — probably dating back to pagan initiation rites.

National Day, celebrated on 10 June, marks the anniversary of the death of Luís de Camóes, considered to be Portugal's greatest poet.

July

The Feira do Carmo is a major festival held in Faro. This fair is a good source for local handicrafts.

The Beer Festival in **Silves** is a predictably merry event, with brass bands and folk dancers, held in the third week in July.

August

The Sardine and Seafood Festival at **Olhão** makes the most of the fact that Portuguese sardines are at their fattest and tastiest during August.

September

National Folklore Festivals, with folk dancing, *fado* and folklore music, are held throughout the Algarve and provide good opportunities to buy local handicrafts.

October

The International Algarve Car Rally, featuring Portuguese and European championships, is held at a different place each year.

The Feira de Santa Iria is a large fair/festival held in **Faro.**

Republic Day: This October Bank Holiday commemorates 5 October 1910 *(see page 19),* when the monarchy was overthrown in Portugal.

2 November

All Souls' Day is taken very seriously. After prayers the women, traditionally clad in black, leave the church laden with chrysanthemums to place on the graves of their loved ones. The chrysanthemum, which blooms in winter, is seen by many as the symbol of life in the darkness of death.

25 December

Christmas Day is traditionally a low-key, strictly religious affair. Only in recent years has Santa come down the chimney. *Bacalhau a Brás* (a dish of cod, egg and potato) is traditionally eaten on Christmas Eve; fowl or mutton are eaten on Christmas Day. 'Christmas Cake' is a type of bread topped with preserved fruit. Custom dictates that whoever gets the slice with the broad bean has to provide the cake next year.

Practical Information

TRAVEL ESSENTIALS

Climate — When to Go

The Algarve has a warm climate with over 3,000 hours of sunshine a year — more than the Costa Brava, Mallorca and the French Riviera. The hottest months are July and August when temperatures rise to 30^0C/86^0F, and recently even as high as 39^0C/102^0F. However, summer temperatures are below the extremes of those in the Mediterranean countries and the sea breezes keep down temperatures in the evenings. The ideal time to visit is spring, before the temperatures soar and the crowds arrive. To see the almond trees in blossom you need to go as early as late January or February, when temperatures are still at their coolest. In April and May the countryside is lush and green with a profusion of wild flowers. Later on the landscape looks very parched and barren. Autumns are mild but recent Novembers have been very wet.

The temperature of the Atlantic tends to be a lot cooler than the Mediterranean. The official temperature of the water in summer is 22°C/72°F, but it feels colder. The west coast waters are the coolest; as you go east the waters warm up by a degree or two.

How to Get There

TAP Air Portugal (tel: 0845-6010932) and British Airways (tel: 0845-7733377) operate a regular service direct to Faro from Heathrow and Gatwick respectively. The BA cut-price offshoot Go operates scheduled flights from Stansted to Faro. Countless charter flights operate from UK regional and European airports. These are far cheaper than scheduled services. Charter flights are conditional on your staying a Saturday night; scheduled flights punish you severely if you don't. From New York there are flights to Lisbon most days of the week, with connecting flights to Faro.

The train journey from the UK is long and more expensive than charter flights. Going by car takes from two to three days. Faro is 2,250 km (1,395 miles) from the Channel ports, but you can reduce journey time substantially by taking the Plymouth to Santander or Portsmouth to Bilbao ferry.

From Lisbon there are frequent flights to Faro. In addition, a rail service covers the whole of the Algarve.

Visas and Passports

Visitors to Portugal from the UK, USA and Australia need only a passport for visits of up to three months.

Other EU residents need only carry an I.D card.

Driving Licences

EU driving licences or international driving licences are valid in Portugal.

Vaccinations

No vaccinations are officially required for visitors from the EU or USA.

Money Matters

The Portuguese monetary unit is the *escudo*, which is divided into 100 *centavos*. The *escudo* is written like a dollar sign ($) between the *escudos* and the *centavos*, hence 80$50 is 80 *escudos*, 50 *centavos*. Bank note denominations are 10,000$, 5,000$, 2,000$, 1,000$ and 500$. There are coins of 200$, 100$, 50$, 20$, 10$, 5$ and 2$. Working in such big sums can be confusing. It helps to remember that 1,000$ equals around £3/US$6 and is called a *conto*.

Travellers' cheques are the safest way to carry money. If lost or stolen they can be replaced (in the case of American Express traveller's cheques within 24 hours, sometimes by courier). In the Algarve, bank exchange rates for traveller's cheques are more favourable than they are for cash. But banks charge a high commission rate on every transaction, so it is cheaper to change one large amount rather than lots of small ones. Eurocheques, with card, are widely accepted in hotels and good restaurants. Automatic cash dispensers are widely available.

Nearly all restaurants and shops change travellers' cheques, but the commission tends to be higher than the bank rate. Major credit cards are accepted by larger hotels, restaurants and shops, and most petrol stations.

Clothing

Take light clothes in summer, plus a jersey or two for cool evenings. In winter it is wise to take a warm jacket or coat, though during the daytime you are likely to need no more than a jersey, if that. Casinos and some luxury restaurants prefer men to wear a jacket and tie. Elsewhere, casual wear is the norm. Whatever time of year you go, remember to take sunglasses.

Electrical Equipment

The supply is 220/240 Volts AC. Plugs have two round pins and most British and American appliances will need an adaptor. The larger hotels will usually supply these.

ON ARRIVAL

Customs Regulations

You may bring as much currency into the country as you wish.

Transport from the Airport

The airport is 7 km/4¼ miles west of Faro and the tourist information office within the building can provide information on transport. The journey by car to the centre takes about 15 minutes. Taxis cost roughly 2,000$. Buses (200$) run roughly every hour in the daytime in summer, but services at weekends are more limited. Car hire companies (both international and local) have branches at the airport. Using the new IP1 motorway, the journey from Faro to Albufeira takes 30 minutes. On the N125, add another 15 minutes or more to that time.

GETTING AROUND

By Car

To cover the itineraries which form the core of this book you require a car. Shop around for the best car hire rates, and beware of the 'extras', particularly insurance. Petrol is cheaper than in the UK, and most of Europe.

It is normally cheaper to reserve a car before you leave home, though the recent downswing in tourism in the Algarve has resulted in a lot of local firms offering very cheap on-the-spot deals. The international car hire companies are inevitably more expensive than the smaller local firms and not always worth the extra. Portuguese national tourist offices can provide you with a list of international and local companies. To hire a car you must be over 23 and have had a licence for at least a year. Valid British, EU, American or international licences are accepted. Check that rates include tax.

Finding your way along the coast presents no problems. The new highway, the IP1, runs from the Spanish border as far as Albufeira, while the old N125 extends the whole length of the Algarve, running more or less parallel to the coast. Side roads from the N125 run south to resorts and beaches, and the signing along here (as opposed to inland) is fairly efficient.

East of Albufeira the traffic jams along the N125 have been relieved by the construction of the IP1 and west of Lagos the road has been widened and improved. However, the N125 highway is still one of the most dangerous in Europe, and it is the subject of a 'zero tolerance' regime. Beware: the police will fine you on the spot for the smallest offence. The main hazard is the unpredictability of Portuguese drivers who overtake on blind bends, fail to indicate and generally lack any sort of road etiquette. Dangers at night are bicycles without lights, horsedrawn carts and inconspicuous locals dressed in black.

Filling up with petrol is easy if you are on the main roads, but petrol stations are sparse in some inland regions. Unleaded petrol (*gasolina sem chumbo*) is now available everywhere.

The main highways have emergency telephones in case of breakdown. Some foreign automobile associations, including the AA and RAC, have reciprocal arrangements with the Portuguese ACP (Automóvel Clube de Portugal), at Francisco Barreeto 26a, Faro, tel: 289-898950.

Before you set out on the itineraries it is useful to know that a *praia* is a beach and a *praça* or *largo* is a square.

Rules of the Road

Speed limits are 120kmh/75mph on motorways, 90kmh/56mph on other roads and 60kmh/37mph in built-up areas. You should carry your driving license and identity papers at all times. Safety belts are compulsory and children under 12 must sit in the back. Drinking and driving is against the law and the alcohol limit is very low, so it is best not to drink at all.

By Bus

It is easy to get around the Algarve by bus. A comprehensive network run by the state-owned *Rodoviária Nacional* covers the whole region, including tiny villages. Fares are very reasonable. For long journeys it is far quicker to use one of the express services run by private companies, but you will need to buy a ticket in advance. Various express coach services run to Lisbon from Faro, Albufeira, Portimão, Lagos and other main centres.

By Train

A train service operates from Vila Real de Santo António in the east to Lagos in the west, stopping off at Tavira, Olhão, Faro, Albufeira and Silves. It is very cheap and quite an amusing way to see some of inland Algarve, but not if you are in a hurry.

Taxis

New Portuguese cabs are cream; older ones are black with a green roof. You can usually find them in the centres of towns and resorts. Elsewhere you will have to call for one. Fares are reasonable by European standards though they tend to be a lot higher south of the N125.

Bike Hire

Hiring a motorbike has its hazards. There are many accidents involving both locals and tourists along the N125. Driving along potholed secondary roads can be dodgy too. Bicycles may be hired in main resorts, but cycling inland up hills is hard work.

By Foot

Getting around town on foot is facilitated by pedestrianised shopping streets. There are some lovely coastal and inland walks, best done off-season or at either end of a hot summer's day. As well as the walks suggested in the itineraries, the following are well worth trying: Barragem da Bravura, 14 km (9 miles) north of Lagos, a large unspoilt reservoir surrounded by wooded hills; the Barragem do Arade, a smaller reservoir northeast of Silves, with beautiful walks all round; the verdant hills of Monchique, where it's noticeably cooler than along the coast; and the west coast, which provides wonderfully bracing clifftop walks.

Maps

With the recent construction of new roads, many maps are out of date. The Bartholomew Leisure Map of the Algarve is the easiest to follow, but the north of the region is only covered by an inset map. The *Automóvel Clube de Portugal* publishes a good tourist map of the Algarve. Free local maps, available at tourist offices and car hire depots, are only sufficient if you are concentrating on the coast.

Ordnance Survey maps of the region, available at McCarta, 122 King's Cross Road, London WC1, are not as accurate as their British equivalents.

WHERE TO STAY

The bulk of accommodation along the coast comprises self-catering villas or apartments. Standards are high by European standards and some of the villas are the height of luxury with marble furnishings, manicured gardens and pools. Some of the most luxurious accommodation lies on the fringes of golfing fairways.

The range of hotels starts with the simple family-run *pensão* (pension or guesthouse) or *residencial* and culminates in five-star luxury. In between and well worth seeking out is the privately run four-star *estalagem*, or inn, which tends to have fewer facilities than a hotel but is cheaper and is far more Portuguese in character; or the *albergaria,* which is very similar to an *estalagem.* The comfortable state-run *pousadas (*equivalent to the Spanish *paradors*) are thin on the ground in the Algarve. There is one set in the hills north of São Brás de Alportel and another on the clifftops in Sagres.

Hotels are graded from one to five stars, but prices are no longer state controlled. You may find that a three-star *pensão* is a lot more appealing and possibly cheaper than a hotel of one star. In high season along the coast, prices of rooms can almost double. If you arrive without a booking, ask to see the room before you take

Monte do Casal hotel

it. This is considered normal practice. Any hotel with three or more stars will probably have its own pool or at least easy access to a beach.

If all official accommodation is taken, enquire locally or at the tourist office about rooms to let in private houses. Staying in a simple room with a local family will cut your costs and improve your Portuguese.

The following are hotels singled out either for their Portuguese character, location, charm or general ambience. The list is by no means comprehensive. Average hotel prices, based on a room for two per night, are 5,000$–9,000$ for 2-star, 7,000–16,000$ for 3-star and 14,000–23,000$ for 4-star. A double room in a 5-star hotel costs up to 40,000$. Continental breakfasts are almost always included in the price of the rooms.

Albufeira

Boa Vista. Rua Samora Barros. Tel: 289-589175/6/7.
Stylish modern hotel with lovely views of the bay from big windows. Situated above the town, with its own pool.
Rocamar. Rua Jacinto D'Ayet. Tel: 289-586990.
Three-star hotel in quiet area a few minutes walk up from the village. Simple but pretty decor. Steps down to the beach.
Sheraton Algarve Pine Cliffs Pinhal do Cocelho Tel: 289-500100.

New luxury hotel, 8 km/5 miles from Albufeira on clifftops with splendid views. Private beach, indoor and outdoor pools, tennis, gym and free use of Golf and Country Club.

Burgau

Residencial Casa Grande Tel: 282-697416.
Faded grandeur. Very informal and quite eccentric, hence popular with artists and writers of all nationalities. Close to the sea.

Faro and Surroundings

Casa de Lumena. Praça Alexandre Herculano, 27. Tel: 289-801990.
Congenial three-star *pensão* occupying old house on a central square. Antique furnishings, restaurant, bar.
Eva. Avenida da República. Tel: 289-803354.
Uninspiring eight-floor block in prime location overlooking port. Roof-top pool, disco, top-floor restaurant.
Monte do Casal. Cerro do Lobo, Estoi. Tel: 289-991503.
Small and exclusive, run by an English couple. Very quiet setting with lovely gardens, pool and fine views. Meals in a converted coach house or on the pool-side terrace. Twelve rooms, including some suites.
La Réserve. Santa Bárbara de Nexe. Tel: 289-999474.
Part of the *Relais et Chateaux* group, hence luxurious and very pricey (double room 36,000$). In extensive grounds, 10 km/6 miles from Faro. Modern apartments with living room, air-conditioning, TV, veranda and south sea view. Large pool and tennis court. International cuisine.

Lagos

Hotel de Lagos. 1 Rua Nova da Aldeia. Tel: 282-769967.
Innovative building a few minutes' walk up from the town centre. Spacious rooms, marble hallways, fine views;

free transport to Meia Praia and hotel beach club.

ALBERGARIA CASA DE SÃO GONÇALO
73 Rua Cândido dos Reis.
Tel: 282-763091.
Charming four-star *albergaria*, converted from an old town house. Full of antiques and character. Every bedroom is different. Breakfast is served on the patio. Closed in winter.

LOULÉ JARDIM HOTEL. Pr. Manuel de Arriaga. Tel: 289-413094.
Modern three-star hotel, with pool.

PENSÃO MAR AZUL. Rua 25 de Abril. Tel: 282-769143.
A rather spartan but cheap and very central pension.

Monchique

ALBERGARIA DO LAGEADO. Caldas de Monchique. Tel: 282-912616.
Comfortable and reasonably priced for this popular spot in the Serra de Monchique. Spotless rooms, tiled floors, restaurant and pool. Sits amidst luxuriant vegetation.

ESTALAGEM ABRIGO DA MONTANHA
Estrada de Fóia. Tel: 282-912131.
Delightful restaurant with rooms on mountainside. Very peaceful with only five rooms and three suites. Prices range from 10,000$–13,000$ for twin with breakfast. Half-board rates available. Good Portuguese cooking.

Penina

PENINA GOLF AND RESORT HOTEL
Tel: 282-415415.
Ranks among the most luxurious hotels of the Algarve. Set in own 146-ha (360-acre) estate, with Olympic-size pool, riding, sauna, shops and immaculate gardens. Free golf for residents.

Praia da Rocha

BELA VISTA. Tel: 282-450480.
Fine old clifftop mansion, looking incongruous among modern blocks. One of the first hotels of the Algarve, built well before the advent of tourism.

Bela Vista Hotel

Traditional decor with fine wood panelling and tiles. The beach lies below.

Sagres

POUSADA DO INFANTE. Tel: 282-624222.
Civilised state-run hotel on clifftops with views across coast to the fortress of Sagres. Marine and Henry the Navigator themes in public rooms. Attractive restaurant serving Portuguese cuisine. Garden with lush lawn, pool and tennis. All rooms have sea views. Ask for one with balcony (no extra cost).

DOM HENRIQUE. Sítio da Mareta.
Tel: 282-620000.
Charming four-star *residencial* on square with sea views. Neighbouring bar can be noisy.

Salema

ESTALAGEM INFANTE DO MAR. Praia de Salema. Tel: 282-690100.
Attractive low-lying hotel up from beach with cool whitewashed walls and tiled floors. All rooms with balcony and sea views. Pool, restaurant.

PENSÃO MARE. Praia da Salema.
Tel: 282-695165.
Modern, reasonably priced and congenial B&B close to the beach.

São Brás de Alportel

POUSADA DE SAO BRAS.
Tel: 289-842305.
State-run 1940s *pousada* 2km (1¼ miles) north of São Brás. Lovely views from terrace and some rooms, and peaceful setting. Variable Portuguese cuisine. Good breakfasts. Wood-burning fires in winter and an outdoor pool in summer.

Tavira

RESIDENCIAL DO CASTELO. Rua Liberdade 4. Tel: 281-323942.
Central, friendly *pensão* almost opposite the tourist office. Comfortable, modern rooms but specify a quiet one at the back.

RESIDENCIAL PRINCESA DO GILÃO.
Rua Borda de Agua de Aguiar 10–12. Tel: 281-325171.
Small, spotless riverside hotel, over the bridge from the main square.

Vale de Lobo

DONA FILIPA. Tel: 289-394141.
Height of luxury and ostentation, next to the golf course. Green fees included in the room rate.

Camping

Camping on the beach is strictly forbidden. For details of official sites ask at any Portuguese tourist office. The Guide to Camping Parks *(Guia dos Parques de Campismo)* has information on 18 official sites in the Algarve, from one to four stars. On a well equipped three-star site, complete with restaurant, pool, tennis, etc, expect to pay around 2,000$ per night for two in high season, including tent and car.

GETTING ACQUAINTED

Information Sources

The following resorts and towns have their own tourist information offices: Albufeira, Armação de Pera, Faro, Lagos, Loulé, Olhão, Portimão, Carvoeiro, Quarteira, Silves, Tavira, Vila Real de Santo António. Free leaflets are available with maps of the resorts and information on the sights to see. Tourist offices stock the *Welcome* magazine, with practical information on the different regions of the Algarve. There's also the monthly *Algarve Gazette* with sections on sightseeing and events along with general features on such subjects as fashion, golf, local news and advertisements galore for real estate. Both are distributed free. The *Algarve Resident,* at 180$, is fairly up-market with features on art, travel, fashion, and luxury homes in the Algarve. The *Algarve News*, a tabloid newspaper which is distributed free, is surprisingly informative for a local rag. It covers both local and national news and provides useful information about upcoming events.

About half the TV shows are American or English. All four channels show English language films in the original versions. Locals glued to Brazilian soaps in cafés are a familiar sight.

Algarve radio stations broadcast news bulletins and musical programmes in English. On short wave you can tune into international programmes from Europe and Voice of America.

The address of the Portuguese National Tourist Office in London is 22/25a Sackville St, London W1X 1DE, tel: (020) 7494 1441, fax: (020) 7494 1868.

Tipping

Although restaurant bills normally include service it is quite common to leave a bit extra, particularly if you think the service warrants it. Hotel bills include service but doormen will appreciate a few *escudos*. If you knock on the door of the local priest to see a church, or the sacristan to go up a tower, it is customary to leave something towards the upkeep of the church buildings. A taxi driver will be delighted with a tip but won't necessarily expect one.

Business Hours

Banks are open Monday to Friday, either 8.30am–3pm or 8.30–11.45am and 1–2.45pm.

Shops are open Monday to Friday 9am–1pm and 3–6 or 7pm, Saturday 9am–1pm. Markets are held from 8am–1pm Monday to Saturday.

Public Holidays

The following days are observed as official public holidays:

New Year's Day	1 January
National Day	25 April
Labour Day	1 May
Camões' Day	10 June
Assumption	15 August
Republic Day	5 October
All Saints' Day	1 November
Restoration Day (Day of Independence)	1 December
Immaculate Conception	8 December
Christmas Day	25 December

Moveable dates are Carnival, Good Friday, Easter Sunday and Corpus Christi.

HEALTH AND EMERGENCIES

Tap water is drinkable but not always palatable. Bottled water is sold everywhere. Ask for *agua mineral,* either *com gas* (fizzy) or *sem gas* (still). Monchique is the local spa. Take it from the springs or drink it ready-bottled.

Emergencies

Dial 112 for police, fire brigade or ambulance.

Hospitals

The hospitals at Faro (289-891100) and Portimão (282-450300) both have a 24-hour casualty department. For less urgent cases there are local hospitals at Lagos, Monchique, Lagoa, Albufeira, Loulé, São Brás de Alportel, Olhão, Tavira, Vila Real de Santo António and a British Hospital in Lisbon.

Welcome magazine prints the telephone numbers of local hospitals and English or English-speaking doctors and dentists. Pharmacies are normally open 9am–1pm and 3–7pm, and work on a rotating basis after hours. The address of the open pharmacy will be listed on all pharmacy doors.

Crime

Portugal is still one of the safest countries in Europe and you are unlikely to come across violent crime in the Algarve. However, there are increasing reports of bag snatching and car thefts, particularly from hired cars in the summer months. Thieves (often from Lisbon or Spain) sometimes work in pairs with two cars and a walkie-talkie device.

It is advisable, therefore, to take elementary precautions. Never leave valuables in the car and make sure any articles you do have are locked in the boot, out of sight. When you hire a car, it is best to get one with a proper boot or a back shelf that will hide possessions underneath.

COMMUNICATIONS

Telephone

Avoid public pay-phone boxes if you can. The coin boxes often need emptying, which means that you won't be able to get through. Instead, make calls from a cafe or bar or buy a prepaid credit card, available from post offices, some shops and cafes. Along the coast over half of the public booths now accept cards.

Alternatively, go to the local telephone office. Here you simply ask for a booth, the operator gives you a line and you can speak for as long as you like. Payment is made at the end of the call. Calls costing over 500$ can be paid for with Visa or Mastercard. The most expensive surcharges of all are levied by hotels, so make calls from a card booth if at all possible.

If you are calling locally remember that all numbers have 9 digits and you have to dial the complete number anywhere within Portugal. The leading '0' has been replace by '2', and area codes have been abolished. If you are calling anywhere outside Portugal, dial 00 for an international line fol-

lowed by the country code (44 for the UK, 1 for the USA). For the international operator call 171. Access numbers for USA phone credit cards are as follows: Sprint: 800-8001871; MCI: 800 80012 31; AT&T: 800-800 1281.

õ or a vowel followed by *m* or *n* in certain positions) are the biggest problems as far as English speakers are concerned.

On the coast English is widely spoken, but north of the N125 you are likely to need at least a smattering of Portuguese. Mastering even a few key words is invaluable.

Post

Opening hours of post offices vary. In large towns and resorts the hours are 8.30 or 9am–6 or 6.30pm from Monday to Friday, 9am–12.30pm on Saturday. Elsewhere they are closed at lunchtime and on Saturday.

Mail can be collected from any post office provided it is clearly marked *Lista de Correios*. You will need your passport as proof of identification. There is small charge.

SPECIAL INFORMATION

The People

The Portuguese are generally good-natured, civil, relaxed and obliging. Not as loud or flamboyant as the Spanish and Italians, they are warmer in character than natives of northern climes and full of generosity. As a race they are very nationalistic. Try to avoid criticism of the country and its people. It is the custom to shake hands upon meeting.

The Language

Knowledge of Spanish or French helps you understand written Portuguese, but the pronunciation, with its elusive nasal intonations and Eastern European-sounding inflections, can be difficult to understand. Nasal vowels (those with a tilde mark such as ã or

Numbers

1	um, uma	**2**	dois, duas
3	trés	**4**	quatro
5	cinco	**6**	seis
7	sete	**8**	oito
9	nove	**10**	dez
11	onze	**12**	doze
13	treze	**14**	catorze
15	quinze	**16**	dezasseis
17	dezassete	**18**	dezoito
19	dezanove	**20**	vinte
30	trinta	**40**	quarenta
50	cinquenta	**60**	sessenta
70	setenta	**80**	oitenta
90	noventa	**100**	cem/cento
1,000	mil		

Days of the Week

Sunday	Domingo
Monday	Segunda-feira
Tuesday	Terça-feira
Wednesday	Quarta-feira
Thursday	Quinta-feira
Friday	Sexta-feira
Saturday	Sábado

Questions

Where is..?	Onde é..?
When..?	Quando..?
How much does it cost?	
	Quanto custa?
Is there..?	Ha..?
Do you have..?	Tem..?
At what time..?	A que horas..?
Do you have a room?	
	Tem um quarto livre?

Essentials

Good morning	Bom dia
Good afternoon	Boa tarde

Good evening	Boa tarde/Boa noite
Good-night	Boa noite
Hello	Olá
Goodbye	Adeus
Please	Por Favor
Thank you	Obrigado
	(spoken by a male)
	Obrigada
	(spoken by a female)
Thank you very much	
	Muito Obrigado/a
How are you?	Como está
Very well	Muito bem
Do you speak English?	
	Fala inglês?
I don't speak Portuguese	
	Não falo portugues
I don't understand	
	Não compreendo
I am lost	Perdi-mi
Yes/No	Sim/Não
Open/Close	Abre/Fecha
Large/Small	Grande/Pequeno
Expensive/Cheap	Caro/Barato

USEFUL CONTACTS

BRITISH CONSULATE: Largo Francisco A Mauricio 7, Portimão, tel: 282-417804.
US EMBASSY in Lisbon: Av das Forças Armadas, tel: 21-7273300.

FARO AIRPORT: Tel: 289-800800.
FLIGHT ENQUIRIES: Tel: 289-800801.
TAP INFORMATION: Tel: 289-800730.
BRITISH AIRWAYS: Tel: 289-803241.

FURTHER READING

Good book stores are thin on the ground in the Algarve and you are best off buying reading matter before you go. Books written specifically about the Algarve are mainly limited to pocket guides which concentrate primarily on the coast.

A good general book on Portugal is *The Portuguese: The Land and Its People*, by Marion Kaplan (Penguin).

It is not a guide book, but a dynamic and readable portrait of Portugal and its people, past and present.

Guide Books

Get to Know the Algarve, Len Port. The complete guide and a very enjoyable read about the Algarve past and present.
Insight Guide: Portugal, Apa Publications, Singapore, Updated 1999. Comprehensive guidebook with background essays and fact-filled information section. Sumptuous photography.
Compact Guide: Portugal, Apa Publications, Singapore, 1997. Easy-to-use portable guidebook.
Compact Guide: Lisbon, Apa Publications, Singapore, Updated 2000. Accessible guide to the capital.

Travel

They Went to Portugal, Rose Macaulay, Penguin. Entertaining account of British travellers to Portugal, from the early crusaders to 19th-century Romantic travellers.

History

A New History of Portugal, H V Livermore, Cambridge University Press, 1976. Comprehensive, and readable.
Prince Henry the Navigator, John Ure, Constable, 1977. Account of the man who initiated the era of discovery.
Portugal, Sarah Bradford, Thames & Hudson, 1973. Interesting account of the nation and the people, from the maritime era to the early 1970s.

Literature

The Lusiads, Luís de Camões. Epic poem (translated) recounting the historical exploits of the Portuguese and the voyage of Vasco da Gama.

Gastronomy

Portuguese Food, Carol Wright, Dent.
The Wines of Portugal, Jan Read, Faber.

Index

ACKNOWLEDGMENTS

Photography	Stuart Abraham *and*
12, 72	Bill Wassman
3, 4/5, 8/9, 26, 75, 82	
86, 87, 89	Tony Arruza
Cover Photography	Guglielmo Galvin/Apa
Handwriting	V Barl
Design	Carlotta Junger
Cover Design	Tanvir Virdee
Editor	Jane Ladle
Managing Editor	Tom Le Bas
Cartography	Berndtson & Berndtson